DIGITAL MARKETING STRATEGY

An Easy-to-use Beginner's Guide to Building Your Brand

(The Ultimate New Passive Income Strategies, Using the Best Tips)

Katherine Spicher

Published by Oliver Leish

Katherine Spicher

All Rights Reserved

Digital Marketing Strategy: An Easy-to-use Beginner's Guide to Building Your Brand (The Ultimate New Passive Income Strategies, Using the Best Tips)

ISBN 978-1-77485-168-5

Table of Contents

Table of Contents

Introduction

Digital marketing is a key tool for businesses to market their products or services. This is not surprising considering that most people spend a lot time on their smartphones.

It's not an assumption that brands and companies don't understand digital marketing. Their entire digital marketing strategy revolves around posting random content on their websites in the hopes of driving organic traffic to their site and increasing sales.

This strategy is no longer efficient. It worked well for the past few decades, but the internet is now crowded. You need a strategy to compete with your competitors. The good news is that not all solopreneurs or businesses have yet switched to a more programmatic and systematic approach to digital marketing. This is an advantage for those who are willing and able to put in the effort to build a strong online presence for their company or themselves.

This book will cover everything you need to learn about creating a strong and effective digital marketing strategy. Each step will have a clear goal: Monetization.

A digital marketer who is skilled at converting clients into customers is an excellent one. This is what separates him from an aspiring entrepreneur. The first person is more concerned with building his personal brand than creating revenue for his business. The second thinks that comments and likes will make them money. Although you must choose the category you want, we can guarantee your business will be able to attract customers like a pro.

Because of this, we decided to write the book. We got tired of being sold expensive programs and books by "Gurus", who promise to give you their "special weapon". Digital marketing is not difficult. It is not hard to work.

However, there has never been a book that covers all the details of this incredible world. We set out to accomplish that feat and leave no stone unturned. This book has all you need to turn your online business into a profitable one.

Chapter 1: What is Digital Marketing?

Digital marketing can be described as any type of marketing that is done online. Digital marketing is any form of marketing that takes place online.

Before we get into the details of how to start digital marketing, let's first understand the basics. This will help you understand where digital marketing is coming from, what it takes, and who can make the most from it. This information will help determine if you are a good candidate for digital marketing. This will help you understand what digital marketing strategies are modern and high-quality, as well as what strategies are obsolete.

How did digital marketing begin?

In 1990, the launch of the first search engine "Archie", the first use of the term "digital marketing" occurred. Developers suggested that people could one day use the internet to market their businesses, by having their business appear on relevant search lists displayed by Archie.

Developers created the first clickable ad banner in 1993. It is similar to the ones that you see today on the internet. These banners were placed at the top of websites, just as they are today. They could be clicked to allow people to instantly visit the company's website. One year later, the first internet transaction was made using an application called "Newmarket" in 1994. Two years later, other search engines were added, such as Yahoo!, LookSmart and HotBot. In 1997, "SixDegrees.com", the first social media site, was launched. In 1998, "Google" was finally launched.

After the launch of all these websites, platforms such as LinkedIn, WordPress and MySpace, Gmail Facebook, YouTube, Twitter and MSN were created. Split testing is a digital marketing strategy that allows companies to launch two campaigns simultaneously to determine what reach their target audience the most. What is Digital Marketing?

Because digital marketing is affordable and the information is easily accessible, it is one of the easiest ways to market your business. Digital marketing can be used to make an income for your business or start a new business.

Digital marketing is much cheaper than traditional advertising, which can run upwards to $250+. It can also earn you decent income in a relatively short time, unlike traditional advertising. There are many stories of people who have succeeded in replacing traditional incomes, or even replacing them 10 times over, within a matter of months to a year. It is important to use your startup budget efficiently and set up the right tools in order to have something you can make money with. This is what you will learn in this book. It means that as long you use these techniques and have some spare time, as well as a few dollars to start your business, you can have everything you need.

Who can use digital marketing?

No matter where you are from or how much money or whether you have a business to sell your goods, digital marketing can be used. Digital marketing can be used if you're willing to learn the basics and find a product or service that you want to sell. Digital marketing is now more accessible than ever. There are many options to start your own business, or find products or services that you want to sell. You can make a living with digital marketing as long as you're able to get in touch with the right companies.

How can I make money with digital marketing?

There are two main ways to make money in digital marketing: selling your products or services or selling the products of others. We will show you how each strategy can help you make an income through digital marketing.

You will need to know what products and services you want in order to make an income selling your own products or services. This is not something you should worry about if you already have a company with products and services. However, if you're just beginning to build a company and selling products or services, then you will need to find something to sell. You can sell almost anything online, as long as your target market is identified and marketed to. You can search for any product or service, digital or physical, and make a market. It is a good idea to research what products and services are most popular at the time to make it easier to sell your products or services. You can easily access a buyer market by following the trends and selling trending products and services to make an income.

You should be aware that offering your own products and services is less passive than the other forms of digital marketing income. You may be required to ship or supply the products or fulfill service requests. This can take a lot of time. You can hire another person to do the job if you have the money, but this will take more work on your part.

You can also market for someone else. This can be done via dropship marketing or affiliate marketing. Dropship marketing is where another company receives and fulfills orders. All you have to do it market for them in order for them to get these orders. You earn an income by submitting customers to your company for purchase. Dropshipping or affiliate marketing can be a great way to make a passive income.

Both marketing strategies can be used with the same digital marketing tools and they both have the potential to generate income. The best one for you will depend on the amount of income you can earn and how much effort and time it will take to accomplish.

Chapter 2: Identifying Income Sources

If you have a company, you will already know your income channels. These are the products or services you offer your customers. However, if you don't have a company, you will need to identify your income channels so you can find out where your customers are making money with your digital marketing business.

You know that you can make money selling your products and services or marketing for others. We will be discussing four income channels that you could explore. Also, we will discuss the pros and cons of each channel so you can choose the right income channel for your business. You will know what to market so you can make a living with digital marketing.

Selling products

The most labor-intensive type of digital marketing strategy is the one that sells products. This is because you need to take into account the effort it will take to manage your inventory. It will be necessary to locate a supplier, order and receive products, store them, and then ship the products once they are purchased. It can be quite time-consuming and may not provide passive income.

Outsourcing much of the work can help you make your product-based retail business more labor-intensive. Amazon FBA allows you to create a business and Amazon will handle all aspects of your inventory. This includes buying the product from a supplier and shipping it to Amazon. You will only need to identify the products that you wish to sell and purchase them from suppliers. Then, Amazon will ship them to your warehouse and their employees will handle the rest. You can also use marketing to increase sales and get your products offloaded faster. This service will require more work because you are outsourcing some of your business's work. If you don't want to take on additional steps and cost, it may not be the best option.

If this is the right path for you, you can still start identifying products to sell online. You will know that you will only be selling your products online, so you can concentrate your efforts on getting people interested in your products. This traditional approach to advertising and retail is what many people find the easiest to understand and makes the most sense.

Instead of using traditional marketing methods, digital products can be created. You can download eBooks, apps or printable sheets to digital products for a variety of purposes. These could be used to color, manage inventory, and more. Digital graphics can be used to create logos, patterns, tutorials or courses that help people learn new skills. You can create a variety of digital products that can be used for digital marketing. Selling digital products is much easier than selling stock. You simply create the digital product online on Shopify or Etsy and then when someone purchases, they will receive an automatic download file. In return for payment. This is a great way to set up a shop online and make money through digital marketing.

Selling services

Selling services is another way to sell digital marketing. This can make it more labor-intensive. You will need to be able to fulfill the services once they are purchased. You can also hire people to fulfill these services for you. In this case, you are more like an agent who recruits and finds work.

This income channel can be used with digital marketing to make a good income, especially if your agent is chosen. You can sell many services online. These services include consulting, teaching new skills or providing the final product of valuable skills like video editing or writing services. This strategy can help you make a steady income online if you possess these skills or are connected to people with them.

Affiliate Marketing

Affiliate marketing is the most passive type of digital marketing. Affiliate marketing is the simplest type of digital marketing. You only need to market products to another company.

Affiliate marketing requires you to have an existing audience and engage online. You can demonstrate to companies that your marketing skills are strong by having a targeted audience. This will allow you to increase the likelihood of you generating sales via digital marketing. This is the best way to reach out to companies offering affiliate marketing deals. You can earn commissions on the sales you make for them.

Affiliate marketing is an option for those who do not have a strong online audience. However, this will require you to choose another avenue. For people without a strong online audience, it is common to join an affiliate company where they can make money. People can buy into an affiliate marketing company and then start marketing for the company. This method can be extremely lucrative, and it often offers a better compensation plan than traditional affiliate marketing agreements. Network marketing companies typically pay more for better performance, which allows you to earn higher levels of compensation within the company. It does limit what you can market to, since network marketing companies don't like when you market for multiple companies simultaneously.

Affiliate marketing has many great benefits. You can become involved with companies and set up automated marketing systems so you don't have to do as much marketing their products on a daily basis. The automated services work in the background, earning you money without your direct involvement. This marketing strategy has been proven to generate passive income of thousands of dollars every month for many people. It is a great strategy to try if you're willing to do the work and put in the effort to make it successful.

Dropship Marketing

Dropship marketing is the last income stream you have to consider online. Dropship marketing is similar in that you market products for another company and they will handle all aspects of stocking and shipping the products. It is however completely different in the way that the business is set-up. Dropshipping is different from affiliate marketing where you only endorse products and use them. Instead of using the product to promote your business, you will need to establish a brand and a website that you can sell products. You will then upload products from another person to your website so people can visit your site and buy the products you are selling. You will be paid a commission and the drop shipping company will fulfill any orders that people have placed through your website.

Although this strategy requires more effort and money to start than affiliate marketing, it is easier than selling products and services. You don't have to manage inventory management or order fulfillment. However, you will need to set up a website and promote your business to others so they can buy from you. You can make a lot of money once you have established your business. People who buy more products will spend more, so you can earn more commissions through affiliate marketing.

How to choose the right income channel for you

The amount of effort that you are willing to invest in digital marketing and sales will determine which income channel you choose. All of the income channels mentioned above will require digital marketing efforts in addition to any additional effort required for fulfillment. Selling products, for example, will require digital marketing efforts as well as the effort to identify, source, manage, and fulfill inventory requests.

It is important to know how much time, money, and effort you are willing to invest in your digital marketing strategy. Affiliate marketing and network marketing are the best income channels for those who want to be as involved as possible but don't want to spend too much on their startup. You might consider selling products and services if you're willing to put in more time, effort, money, or time.

Once you have determined the right income channel, it is time to start learning about how that channel works and who can help you set it up. If you are interested in becoming an affiliate marketer, then you must start building your network and find companies you want to market to so you can make an income. If you are looking to sell products, then you should start researching the products that you want to market and then identify sources from which you can buy those products. It is important to identify all people or companies involved in your chosen income stream so you can have the resources and information to start.

Chapter 3: Product Research

There are millions of products to choose from. It's nearly impossible to find something you like.

This is why I developed my own criteria to choose a product for YouTube video reviews.

It's personal, and you don't need to do it to make money.

If you are a novice and don't know where to begin, this will save you time and effort when researching products.

It is important to identify the type of product that you are searching for.

Because they guide you to your destination, goals and targets are essential.

These are my criteria.

Before I review a product, I strive for at least 4 of 5.

FAVORITE FIVE

#1 - The Price

I prefer products priced between $50 and $1,000.

Amazon offers up to 10% commission, and I love to make as much as possible.

You can sell semi-expensive items so that you don't need to sell hundreds of units in order to make money.

#2 - A great product (4.5+ stars).

Also, I want at least a 4.5 star average rating.

Never sell anything just to make a commission.

It must be a good product. Amazon stars are a good indicator of product quality.

#3 - Substitute/Complementary/Variations

This is how you can make 2-3x more money with less effort.

Give them options.

There should be variations.

Other related products should also be promoted.

Complementary products are also needed.

In case they don't like the one that you are promoting, it is a good idea to give them alternatives.

Each of these three options is acceptable, but the combination is best.

#4 - 50-150 Reviews

Affiliate marketing is your first attempt at affiliate marketing. I suggest that you promote products with little competition.

I believe 50 to 150 reviews is the ideal price point.

#5 - It is something you already have or someone you know already has/uses it.

It would be a benefit if someone you know or you have used the product before.

You will have more hands-on experience, and be able do a better job of reviewing.

You can have a slide presentation, but not the product. The best reviews include one that includes a demo or a review with the product being displayed.

(Don't let it stop you from reviewing the product again. Slides are fine too.

First, I suggest that you browse through different categories while still keeping your criteria in mind.

Let's do a real example shall we?

This product falls under the Camping & Hiking category.

#1 - The Price

It costs around $40

Although it is not quite the $50 minimum target, it is close enough.

This is for the purposes of the criteria. I will assign it an X.

#2 - A great product (4.5+ stars).

It has 4.5 stars, so it is good.

#3 - Substitute/Complementary/Variations

Yep, there are lots of substitute/complementary and there's even a variation available.

We can sell many different bags, and also lots of accessories related to hiking.

We can sell gear, shoes, water bottles and emergency kits.

#4 - 50-150 Reviews

At the moment, there are 65 reviews.

#5 - It is something you already have or someone you know already has/uses it.

This bag is a great value for money. It is something I highly recommend to my fellow beginner hikers.

I scored 4 out 5 so that's enough.

Next, create a video review that potential buyers can see.

P.S. P.S. - Your affiliate links can be found in your account by searching for the ASIN of the product or the product name.

Chapter 4: Ways To Boost Your Business Profits With Digital Marketing

Ever wonder if the advertisement for your favorite collection will appear on the internet? You can purchase an item, but then you get an email saying "You have an unsheet product in your cart." Ever wonder why so many websites are linked to the same companies, yet only a few appear on Google's first page search? While there are many possibilities, only a few people are able to explain how this mysterious phenomenon could exist. Digital marketing is the answer to all of these "you've yet" questions.

All types of businesses have embraced digital marketing as the future of business. This is a set of tools and techniques that help to promote products and services on the Internet. Digital marketing and PROFIT really make it possible. Small businesses as well as large corporations have the same goals for their success. On the digitalization journey, both advertisers and businessmen know the world just as well as their clients.

They must also follow the recommendations of customers and not just follow their forms. Sometimes, internet marketing is referred to digital marketing.

1. Online presence

Your main goal is to establish your company online. The company can be displayed on social media platforms and Web sites. This is also called Business Branding. This is the best platform for working in an environment with more than 465,000,000 internet users. Smartphone is another technology that allows users to easily gather information and purchase products or services.

You will use the Internet's power to make your business magical. If you are looking to make significant progress, consider creating your own website or listing your organizations on social media platforms. Don't forget to respond to all comments and questions on the various online platforms. This helps you make a positive impression on each one.

2. 2. Get the Social Media Advertising

Advertisements

Facebook has many marketing options. You can use them to convert people or get more likes for your product.

Similar to Instagram, we can see how the younger generation of more than 700 million active users has flocked onto this social media platform. Advertisers are slowly able to post their ads using filtered photos. The natural way to share brand content is Instagram.

3. Click to Pay

PPC is the best platform to make purchases or request information. PPC is a great way to get your company noticed. At least 10-15% of those who click on sponsored ads will lose their job. Many PPC companies provide services to manage your PPC program, if you don't feel comfortable managing the camps yourself or are unable to hire PPC specialists.

This is crucial because Google Adwords, which offers a wide range of options from search to video and even re-marketing, is your best friend.

The platform allows the client to reach millions of potential clients by offering a variety of options.

4. SEO

SEO is a valuable marketing tactic that has captivated marketers. SEO is an advertising-based marketing strategy to increase traffic and revenue for natural products. SEO is the most cost-effective, but not the fastest way to market your business online. It allows you to reach new markets that you didn't know were possible.

According to the report 75% of Google Apps will not get past page 1. This means that you won't be able to get the visibility you need to generate revenue. You can still use SEO tools for organic search.

5. 5.

Today, video is the most effective way to communicate the brand's message. Over 5 hours of internet time is spent watching and buying video content. Advertisers can be confident that mobile video ads will account for 69% of all internet traffic by 2020. Mobile video ads will grow five times faster than desktops or web landing pages and will convert 800% more. This is huge and sensible.

Many businesses believe that video content is a better way to communicate their brand message than text. Video content has more imagery and a human touch than other methods of content sharing.

6. Digital Social Media Marketing Additional Focus

Facebook, a social media giant has released 556 million digital daily active users. This indicates a 49 percent annual growth. This converts to 945 million monthly active internet users, which indicates a 39 percent increase in users year-on-year.

This is a clear indicator of the impact of mobile social marketing. It should result in more content being created that matches the social media trends and local advertising targeting mobile social media users. Mobile phones are the best source of advertising and contact.

7. Email marketing should be intensified

It's not just email for official communication. There are other aspects to it. Your conversions will be greater if you are proactive and focused. You can gain a lot from the information you have about your customers in your Ecommerce business. It would be a shame if your shopping cart was abandoned. But how can you reverse this trend. You can continue to remarket (a principle of digital marketing) by emailing those items that were left in your basket.

Email Marketing allows you to create a series of emails once a cart has been removed. This results in more sales. You will receive three emails, one directly, one 24 hours later, and one week ago. The most efficient. It is also a backup source for consumers.

8. 8.

You can increase your brand's visibility by creating appropriate promotional or company content. These contents can be found in forums, video clips, testimonials and interviews, as well as material from the website, graphics, images, and other formats.

Start by posting content to blogs that are in the same field as yours to increase traffic and visibility. Advertising is good when it reaches millions of people. Advertisers often overlook the fact that the content you share with your customers can determine the quality of your business.

9. Monitor your behavior and track your achievements

While exploring different digital marketing strategies is great, if you don't keep track of your contributions and promotions it won't be beneficial. After testing, you should evaluate what you can do about it. Which apps are generating more traffic? Which should be your focus? All these results can make a huge difference in your dream of a large business. For example, you will find out how and where people found their stores via Google search and other search consoles.

Facebook Insights, Ad Manager and Facebook Insights can show you the age, location, relationship status and preferences of your customers and fans. Social media listening apps will help us understand what is important to our customers and how we can improve our products and services. These resources will help you gain insight into the demographics and psychography of your audience to get a better idea of what is most important and fascinating.

10. 10.

You can build your company's credibility by adopting a virtual marketing campaign. If you visit other media-related websites, and make a strong pitch, you might submit a story about your company or feature a CEO in blog posts. Your exposure will increase over the next year if more people tweet about your business and mention your name.

Chapter 5: Best Practices

The social media campaign is a company within the company. As you would with a start-up company or large internal initiative, create a project charter as well as a business plan for your social networking program. This is important for the following reasons:

Social media is still a relatively new medium. If you don't record your goals and metrics in writing, they will not be accepted by the entire business.

Because of the rapid pace of change and the proliferation of new media channels and tactics, it is important to set goals and stay focused on achieving them.

Most of the people reading this book have a social media company network. But, I think that very few people have a written strategy. While I don't mean to suggest that you go back and rewrite your strategy, I believe you should.

In the past decade, social networking has evolved into a powerful communication and innovation tool. It is difficult to imagine any corporation or entity today without a social networking strategy. But it was hard to imagine individuals using social networking to promote their businesses in the early days. Many people are suspicious of social media sites and view them as something their adolescent relatives do. Skeptics considered social media to be a waste of time and effort.

This lack of respect for social media may be why many social media proposals fail. Yes, teens and twentysomethings use social media. However, they still have credit cards and use the Internet to drive cars. Do we need to take credit cards, the Internet and cars seriously? It is not. However, the social media mistakes made by people can be easily avoided if they take social media seriously.

Here's a tip for approaching social media: Any information that is shared between these networks has potential. It is not easy to manage any type of marketing, even in this brave new world of social media. It is difficult to overcome the barriers created by the self-proclaimed "gurus" in social media who claim to have the key to this new media. They will sell you their secrets for a very small fee. We are social media writers and want to share a real, honest view of it with you.

Appreciation, hard work, and awareness of the platform is the only way to be successful in social media. You need a solid strategic plan if you want success.

Make a Calendar

Remember that content is the king. From the very beginning of the internet, this has been true ever since. A blog, podcast or social network is what people want for quality content.

However, content must be cohesive and in collaboration. Online updates must have a rhythm and a set schedule. It is not possible for a writer to just slap content onto his blog, Facebook, or elsewhere, and then leave it there for months. They won't be there at regular times that the user can trust. It's all about consistency in blogging.

You can set a schedule and post on specific days. A calendar with a schedule that lists the days and times you will post new content is a great way to manage all your content, including tweeting, blogging, and Facebook posting.

Your calendar should include the topics and recurring columns that you post on your blog. Your calendar should indicate that you post on Mondays and Wednesdays on Facebook and blogs, and Twitter and Pinterest on Tuesdays and Fridays. Once you have an editorial calendar, make sure to stick to it. You will need to plan how many posts you intend to create original content to market your job, and how many educational content.

However, don't let your original plan become your slave. You shouldn't make it your daily routine. Allow for flexibility in your editorial calendar to accommodate new news and issues. You don't want to do this just for traffic, although some people do. But you also want to be able take advantage of these opportunities when you have something to share about a current topic or trend. Keywords will be searched by people, so it is important to keep up with the latest developments in writing and publishing.

A structured approach to content management is easier for authors than a chaotic strategy. With a regular editorial calendar and multiple outlets, it will quickly become a routine.

Before you post something, think about what you are thinking before posting it

When you develop a social media site, you create a name. Your brand is what you do, and it communicates to your readers your credibility as an author. Although it takes time to build a strong brand, there are many things that can go wrong. Snarky comments or other humor can backfire big time, so it is worth looking at the update before it goes live and trying to evaluate it critically. Ask yourself: "Could this not be the right way to go?" You can post it if you aren't sure. Be prepared for negative reactions. Comedy can be hard on social media.

However, controversy is easy to find. You might be impressed by something in the headlines, a Twitter exchange, or an

Instagram photo. But before you get too passionate about a cause, ask yourself "Is this argument worthwhile?" Are both sides fully understanding you? Are you able to spend the time listening and discussing opposing views? Are you under pressure and want to stay focused? Do you have the guts to accept a negative response if you get involved in a heated discussion?

"Actually, when you read the post that you wrote, think about whether it is okay to share it with others. Your network may be made up of followers or friends, but it isn't as intimate as you think. You should consider the consequences of every update you make before breaking glass or pressing the red button in an emergency.

Positive thinking is key

Before you hit send, here's another rule: Never lose heart.

As a professional on social media, you don't have the luxury to whine, lament or go on rants. (Depending on the topic, a rant can be fun. Pip gained a lot of attention on her blog when she laughed at the trend of book covers featuring characters with their heads cut out. Many authors have built a community around the positive message they send, whether that be writing tips or lessons learned from their books on the road. People are tired of negativity and skepticism in their everyday lives. It is possible that they don't want to hear this from authors, especially if it is someone with whom they are interested in social media.

Reflect on your lessons learned and the things you want to share. Be kind, charming, funny, and loving. These qualities will help you get along with readers.

Social media is something you do because you like it. It's not an obligation. Nobody wants to read someone else's blog. Twitter is fun because you are having fun and not because it's something that you have to do. Social media can be a great way for you to connect with other people who are doing the same thing as you. It's also a great place for you to communicate with your audience. You will notice that I said to speak, not shout.

How do we distinguish between what is actually happening and what is being posted on the Internet or on social media? The truth is that social media is real. This is not an illusion. We must treat online information as if it were real. This isn't A Game of Thrones. Online, you can be amazing.

Social Media Strategy

Marketing Zen Community created an "ACT" structure to help you create a social media and online strategy. It stands for Attract, Convert and Transform ",--, which I consider a useful structure to position an online business.

Attract: You must be distinctive in a competitive field to attract potential prospects. Your brand should have a strong value proposition and worthwhile material.

Convert: Improve the design and user interface of your website and social media in order to convert visitors to customers.

Transform: Develop a genuine personal relationship with your customers or clients. It shouldn't be a transaction to do business with you. It should be a relationship with your brand that fosters loyalty and encourages brand advocacy.

This is a great way to assess your business strategy, social media programs, and website presence. Social media marketing is a strategy to increase the communication between the company's audience and the company. Actively cultivate your audience to inspire them to become loyalists and customers.

One Channel, Many Functions

Social media can be used to expand and enhance virtually everything your corporation or company does today, whether it's marketing, market research, customer care, investor relations, or human resource program.

Companies can use social media to accomplish many functions.

Support for the consumer

Engaging clients and building brand equity

Promotion and acquisition of clients

Green Mountain Coffee Roasters is a company where I work with fellow marketers to discuss the place of social media in our integrated promotions calendar. This calendar lists the major promotional activities, seasonal holidays, new product and category releases for the entire year. Any advertising campaign is worth a coordinated effort by multiple marketing platforms: e-mails, direct mail, paid searches ads and online banners;

affiliate marketing; press releases; and messaging on the website.

Social is an integral part of the marketing mix. We announce major promotions and product launches on Facebook, Twitter, our blog, and on Twitter. You can also broadcast the message to other niche channels or networks depending on the promotion, such as YouTube, Foursquare and Pinterest.

A strong social media presence is essential for any organization who wants to establish a personal connection with their audience. They must agree to the following four conditions:

Customer-oriented community that combines responsiveness, personality, authenticity, and professionalism. It is important to respond to customer concerns, grievances and feedback immediately, much like you would in your e mail and call center for outbound customer service. You can also identify the "influential", which are your most loyal brand advocates. They will help you in many ways.

You plan material in the same way a newspaper publisher would. While you are on social media, it is important to have a schedule for Facebook, Twitter and your blog. This will keep your page current and your brand front-and-center in the activity streams of your followers and fans. Remember that 90% of your followers will not return to your site if they only see updates from your feed. Your content plans will include the things you want to share in social media, and promotions and activities you plan to offer your audience.

Promote your space in society. If you don't spend time and money thinking about how to promote your space, they won't come. I'll explain in detail how to drive traffic to your social networks accounts using paid ads, cross-network promotion, and "earned media".

To attract new members to the group, a roadmap for retention. Social media's greatest asset is also its Achilles heel: its enormous and growing size. The sheer volume of followers, tweets and fan pages generates a huge overload. This means that your followers will have very little interaction online with you. Facebook and other social media platforms are not meant to be used as a tool for trolling or hitting potential clients with sales pitches. Social media is a great way to meet your customers, reward their loyalty and gain insight into your business and its inner workings. You can make them feel valued and unique.

I will be discussing advanced social media strategies, retention methods such as "surprise delight", loyalty badges and sweepstakes, feedback campaigns, ambassador services and "gamification" and other topics. These tools will allow you to increase the speed of your social media program, so that it is more user-friendly and attracts new members.

Listening

There are many. Before you get into social media, it is important to understand the meaning of the organization and how it can be translated into the world. However, the approach will also require an external focus. This means that you need to listen to your customers.

The best thing for your corporate social media program is to be better at listening. You can keep up with the conversations on social media about your brand, industry and competitors using social media tracking tools like Tweetdeck, Tweetdeck, SocialMention or Hootsuite. Or simply do daily Twitter searches. You will discover the hot topics and the most influential people in your culture and the wider social sphere by listening to your audience.

Plan

Many elements are involved in social media strategies that have high impact. They can be found in both the traditional media and in the social media world. These campaigns will involve players in the legal, customer service, marketing and operations departments. These campaigns include the implementation and maintenance of technology.

A social media program requires disciplined preparation. Here are some of the processes you might need to use:

Plan for daily community management staffing

Monthly publishing schedules

Customer insights, research, and survey projects

Campaign strategy and promotions briefs

Production briefs and creative design

Technology requirements: Writing, vendor selection, inhouse development, user experience testing, acceptance testing (UAT), testing/debugging

Budgeting and reporting

Participate in a Blog Tour

If done right and in a mutually beneficial manner, there are many activities that can help you introduce your words to new readers. These events can also help you build a solid evergreen content backlist. These blog posts can be quickly repurposed for your blog by being redesigned, updated, or republished. You can wait up to six months to repurpose blog posts. It's the best way to keep good ties with other bloggers.

Blog tours are where you appear on a variety of blogs to guest blog, and maybe even share a common theme. Other bloggers will visit your site at least once a week to discuss topics they are interested in or those you have suggested. To make tours successful for all involved, bloggers should exchange material.

Original

Unique from blog to blog

Fall within 500-1000 words

While some bloggers may not be able to post comments from others immediately, if everyone participates on time, the evergreen content will grow dramatically. This allows you to choose from a wider range of posts that can be reused on your blog or as guest posts.

High Quality Content

Although content can come from many sources, quality should be the main focus of your content. What determines content quality? Although subjective, it is important to be concise, clear, edited, well-researched, and provide quality content. It is common to believe that content posted for the sake is more important than the actual value of the content. However, since your posts are an expression of your work, they are significant.

What do people look for in quality content?

Punctuality

When news about your company breaks the news, you have approximately twenty-four hours to create, edit and deliver a blog post. Your comments must be posted within one week (roughly five days) of the topic. People are looking for angles and stories on this topic at the moment of breaking news. By tapping into the news items' timeliness, you increase the chances of other blogs picking it up and syndicating it. Don't wait too long and you will lose the opportunity to grab the story and drive traffic.

Cross Promotions

From the moment a blog post goes live, Facebook and Twitter should be your first point of promotion. These posts can feel cold, even though automated tools like the WordPress Social plug in that broadcasts updates to your blog are readily available. Follow a flowchart to create a new, original tweet or post that you can add to your blog. This allows the networks to know that you manage an account. It also lets them know that your content is fresh whenever there is overlap.

Cross-Referenced

Your words reflect your character, so linking back to your blog posts with references is a smart move. This is a great way to start the conversation about sharing resources and connecting back to them. Analysts will ask questions about the sources or initiate discussions about the cited resources. Sharing links can attract traffic to your website depending on how generous and respectful the website is. Cross-referencing is an excellent technique to create traffic to your blog.

Visualize whenever possible

A good photo attracts attention. All users engage more with photos than text-only posts across all channels. Tumblr and Pinterest are two examples of sites that focus primarily on images. However, tweets and posts can be more popular if they include a photo. Remember: Pictures are the best for blog posts!

But, it can backfire on your reputation if you use other people's pictures. While you may enjoy sharing Tom Hiddleston memes on social media, if you're a professional trying maintain a good online reputation, it is a bad idea.

Remember that you can't copy another meme and put your website URL on it, as we have discussed in previous chapters. Similar to blog content that is not attributed, when the source of the content is omitted, "scraping", occurs. Posters tag the corresponding content with their page, giving the impression that their original content is the shared content. You can make it come back to you by making someone else's content your own.

If you are making your own photo, it is best to stick with the one you have taken. Depositphotos.com has stock photography. These photos can be used for a small investment. If you're making your own cover, stock images can also be repurposed.

Cultivating and Pursuing "Influential"

They can be ambassadors, tastemakers or connectors. Some members of fan groups are more active than others, have better reputations and may have a greater readership of blogs or print media. Their views are more influential and have greater impact.

These powers are especially useful for a niche-focused, younger audience. As you build and grow your social network, don't blindly ask anyone you meet. Do your research.

These are some thoughts about how Twitter can identify and develop prominent members of groups:

You can search for people who are tweeting about your company, products or market, competitors, or the topic in which you specialize. There are already many experts in your market on Twitter. Follow them.

Keep following people who are experts in your field for at least five weeks, and keep looking until you find at least 50.

Make a list of the top 10 to 20 people who are most likely to become ambassadors for your brand. These will be your Twitter followers that:

Naturally, I did not need to be prompted to talk highly about the brand.

Tweet often with authority, control, and personality. Do it well. They might be behind the trending topics and hashtags in your industry.

You should have many fans. These followers should be involved in your company; they are active on Twitter and well-followed. This is the impact on your network!

Connect with these core Twitter community members regularly by using @ responses and retweets.

Post your tweets and establish yourself as an expert in your field. Once you start following them, you will see some star Twitter group members follow you. Others won't recognize you unless you reply to @ retweet.

You can cultivate it through constructive back-and forth until you have the beginnings to a friendship. Ask them if you can support them. My experience has been positive. We rewarded them with surprise and delight promotions promising free products and reached out with feedback requests.

These are the reasons why you should focus your micro-attention on the core people who make up your Twitter followers:

This is the best way to build a community that's worthy of the label. Not just a list of Twitter handles with no faces, but a core group who feel connected to your brand and organization's greater purpose.

Your followers' passion and subsequent link to your posts means that your posts will be more likely to get retweeted and responded to. This partnership increases the reach and is a way to organic growth.

These are other ways to communicate with influential Facebook users:

When choosing administrators for your Facebook fan pages, make sure you have a range of people that are well-known in your industry. Although they may be using their personal profiles, sometimes it is better to have separate business profiles so that they can use for their business persona.

Administrators can interact with business partners, journalists, opponents, journalists, and prominent clients on Facebook. These relationships may not be personal, but should be professionals.

Administrators would then state that the page is similar to other peers.

As a social media manager, you will need to tap into your customer base and contacts within the industry to send an e-mail to let them know that your page "likes". These are your top clients and people you have already met, who you want to connect with on Facebook. The goal is to build a strong online community of brand advocates and fans.

Hashtags Are Important

This functionality was first introduced to Twitter by social media site, but Instagram, Facebook and Pinterest now have the ability to tap into hashtags' search and trend capabilities.

Hashtags (#), which are tracking tools, allow you to identify posts and updates in any search engine. The hashtag was first used on Twitter by Chris Messina, who tweeted "How do I feel about # (pound) being used for groups" on August 23, 2007. Similar to #barcamp [msg]?

Yes, the first hashtag update was all about hashtags.

There are many ways hashtags can be used. They can be used to express a mood, commemorate a special occasion, or even to mention a joke line. The following are the best ways to use hashtags as writers:

If a new title is being developed or a project is in the works:

While working in a genre:

Tweets that relate to a book or series:

When interactive appearances or ads are identified:

Special occasions such as book festivals or conventions:

You can track trends and conversations through social media sites by using hashtags. You'll also get views from people you don't know. You can follow and join a conversation using hashtags, provided that participants use the same hashtag frequently in discussions. This is true regardless of whether you're using the official Twitter app, checking all Instagram photos with a tag, clicking a tag in an update on Facebook or Google+.

Although not all posts need hashtags, they are essential for certain occasions, current events and special moments.

Book Events and Engagements

A hashtag is a great way to let people know you are attending book festivals. Before you arrive, find out if the event has an official hashtag. Most events have one because they want to show potential sponsors. You can also persuade other writers and your network members to use it. When creating an official hashtag, keep it simple and concise.

Promoting Online Community

Facebook offers three main ways to grow your audience.

Invite friends

Share your page

Advertise on Facebook for a salary

These are listed in order of scalability. Although inviting a few hundred friends is a great start, it's only a beginning. You can share your impact by sharing. This allows you to post on your timeline, on a friend's timeline or in private messages about your website. These strategies are great for getting a group started, but they don't scale. You need to be careful about what you share with whom and how you do it. Do not spam your friends!

With the alpha community, you now want to grow a loyal fan base. Critical mass is when the number of "friends" of your fans reaches the million mark. You can post and your community will grow by hundreds of followers per day. What is the reason? If your posts are provocative and engaging, you will get a lot of comments and likes. These comments and "likes", are sent to all Facebook friends. The same applies to Twitter posts that have been retweeted frequently.

Online group promotion best practices:

Next, make sure to display the logos for Facebook, Twitter and Google+

prominently on any website. Although subtle footer icons have become a common practice, I urge you to think larger. Redbox is an example of this, where it devotes approximately four inches of 20 percent of its footer space to large, eye-catching icons that can be used for Facebook, Twitter and Text Club SMS as well as the iPhone and Android smartphones. A call to action ('Stay In Touch') as well as a customer benefit proposition ("Preview & Reserve Movies!") are important. Redbox includes these features.

You can use widgets or an API (application programming interface) to include certain icons. This will ensure that users don't have to leave your site to "like," "pin", or "follow" you.

The e-mail newsletter footer or header should contain the same logos as the promotions that you send to your home e mail list. Don't forget to include the same logos in automated transactional notifications such as delivery confirmations or promotional e-mails.

Include social media URLs in your catalogue, sales collateral, and other direct mail.

Do something new and different from the norm early on. This will help you get noticed in the media and word-of-mouth. It's hard to be catchy without being gimmicky. However, I love new advertising campaigns that break through the noise and celebrate and reward community development online.

Be Remarkable

In other words, what makes a social media advertisement virally successful is very similar to what makes a brand successful. Frank Goedertier is a professor of marketing and brand management at the Vlerick Leuven Gent School of Management. He is also a visiting scholar at Kellogg School of Management. These qualities are essential for a successful social media campaign. These qualities are essential for a social media strategy that is successful, just like a brand.

Memorable

Meaningful

Likable

Transferable

Protectable

Authentic

Simple

Flexible

Social media is a distraction-laden plethora with triggers. With nearly a billion users and a bias towards fluffy diversions. Particularly, it focuses on the three most important qualities of your campaign: memorable, important, friendly.

Consider Seth Godin, the marketing strategist and author best-selling business books. His constant call to excellence is what you should be thinking about. Although it is not easy to follow the order, it is the best thing.

Only the extraordinary, the thing worth talking about, is going to work.

It is heartening to know that certain brands have a special relationship with their customers. There is a lot of hype and speculation surrounding social media. Social media marketing at its best allows brands to be human and connect with consumers' needs, wants, and beliefs.

Target, for example, launched a back to school season with a charity campaign that targeted American moms directly: Target's Facebook page asked its 16 million followers to "Help us give up $2.5 million to schools."

To cash in on the social network effect, you must understand these key rules:

Your brand should have something unique to stand out.

Social media campaigns must capture the imagination and passion of your followers.

It is important to make sharing easy and fun. You should make participation enjoyable and even addictive by putting out a clear call for action, offering rewards or incentives, as well as providing an enabling feedback loop (or "gamification") of some sort.

Seek Out Your Audience

Every novel has a target audience, but they won't be knocking on your door. You have to find your audience and get to them. Consider yourself and the book you are writing. Which is the best place to be?

Look at the genres that are being written about if you don't already have an idea. Do they seem to have success on these channels? Start building your readership in these areas.

Make a plan

Social media failure is most often caused by jumping on to sites without knowing what you should do. Social networking isn't something you do just because everyone else does it. It's something you do because it is important for you to accomplish.

When you start a blog, think about how many posts you will be writing. Facebook is a great way to promote your blog. What is the maximum amount you can post to Facebook or Twitter? Do you plan to expand beyond these three platforms and use Tumblr instead? Google+ Which will be your voice? Is your voice going to be business-oriented or will you be expressing your personal thoughts? Your online platform will become more organized if you have a strategy.

These tips are a great starting point for social media campaigns. These tips can be applied to your network to help you grow your platform, make your signal more reliable and powerful, and to make your connections easier. Social media can be used to improve and create your brand. Social media can help you identify your brand.

The scary thing about brands is their fragility and vulnerability to harm. It is important to understand what social media is all about. With the right approach, you can avoid many of the mistakes.

Chapter 6: What is Digital Marketing?

What can digital marketing do for your business?

Digital Marketing is a term that has existed since the early 2000s. Digital Marketing is a practice that has existed for over 100 years.

Digital Marketing is a complex subject that requires a lot of research and learning. Digital Marketing is not for everyone. Your strategy should be tailored to your business, clients, and products.

This chapter will explain briefly what Digital Marketing is, and how you can get the most out of it.

Let's now define digital marketing.

Digital Marketing refers to using digital platforms to attract clients to your products and services. This is how I put it.

Digital marketing can take place online and offline. However, this chapter will be devoted to online digital marketing.

Digital Marketing can be described as a broad term that can be divided into seven main categories.

These are the 7 types of digital marketing

Search Engine Optimization (SEO)

Search Engine Marketing (SEM)

Content Marketing

Social Media Marketing (SMM)

Pay-per-click Advertising (PPC)

Affiliate Marketing

Email Marketing

Each category will be covered in more detail later in the book. But for now let's focus on 5 benefits of digital marketing. Although there are many other benefits, these five are my favorite.

Digital Marketing: The Benefits

Results can be measured

You can't measure the number of people who see your flyers or billboards. Digital marketing channels allow you to track and manage how many people reach you, convert to clients and continue to market your services and products to those who are interested.

Digital Marketing is Flexible

Prospects are different. Your marketing message must be adaptable to reach all kinds of prospects. Digital marketing allows you to easily modify and adjust your message to reach different prospects.

Digital Marketing is Cheap

Digital marketing can be cheaper than traditional marketing and it can fit any budget. Digital marketing can be a boon for small and medium businesses, as well as large corporations.

You Can Reach A Larger Audience

Your audience can be anywhere because online digital marketing uses the internet. It is powerful to reach a global audience with online digital marketing. Traditional marketing is limited to a particular geographic area or target audience. This will impact your revenue.

You Can Improve Conversion Rates

The purchasing process is made so simple by digital marketing. With just a few clicks, your clients can purchase a product via an email link on your website or blog. Your clients will be able to purchase products online without the need for a physical shop. This will increase your conversion rate.

These benefits are a dream come real for business owners, I'm sure. You will be amazed at how many business owners prefer traditional marketing methods to digital. Why? They don't know how digital marketing works. We will be discussing how digital marketing works, and how to create a digital marketing strategy that suits your business.

Chapter 7: Tips And Techniques To Get More Leads

Yes, leads can be improved by 10x. If you receive two leads per week, your inbound marketing program will be active. You have 20 leads per week if you get 20 leads per month. If you receive four leads per month, that's 40 leads. This is a reasonable goal that we have set for many of our customers over the past 14 years.

Many business owners, CEOs, and VPs have tried out inbound marketing, but not the results they were expecting. It is not as easy as it appears. It isn't easy but it is rewarding.

If these tips and tricks are implemented correctly and optimized, they will multiply your inbound leads by 10 times.

Marketing is a mathematical calculation which simplifies the process. We've been doing it for years. If you want to increase your leads, you need to move two numbers: site visitors and sitewide conversion rates.

3.1 Search Organically

If people can't find you on Google, Yahoo! or Bing, your business won't be found. If people search for keywords relevant to your business, but not your prospects, you are missing out. If your website isn't responsive, people will search for it on their phones. Your business shouldn't be visible.

It can be time-consuming and difficult to rank your website pages on Google and other search engines. This requires a variety of strategies, including content marketing and social media, website architecture, blog, optimization of conversion rates, and content marketing. All of these areas should be integrated. To determine which areas are working, you should monitor your organic visitors metrics and rank.

Do you know how many leads organic traffic has brought to your site over the last 30 days? Do you know how many organic visitors have visited your site in the past 30 days? These numbers can be compared to the last month. These numbers need to be cooled. These metrics will not help you see improvements. Without this effort, you won't see a 10-fold increase in your productivity.

To increase search engine traffic, you can increase the number of articles in your blog. You can make search results more relevant by including keywords, phrase and query phrases in your blog plan. This will increase your visitors and help you rank better in search engines. You should also examine the structure of your website. You can easily change URL naming conventions and this will have an effect on search results. Google considers it more valuable if the query is replaced with the service page.

The Google algorithm recently changed the way pages are displayed. When people find your link, they should convert to your landing pages. This signalizes Google that the visitor found what you are trying to sell, which improves your rank. Conversion is an important aspect of search. It is crucial to connect all strategies strategically.

Organic search is the best long-term strategy for lead generation. It can be hard to know where to start with all the factors that influence how Google ranks your website in SERPs (search engine result pages). Local SEO optimization is something I believe a major player in Lead Generation. Word Stream reports that 72 per cent of local searchers visited a store within five miles of the location they were searching.

Local SEO helps your business reach the community and find customers when they need it most. Mobile is still the dominant market. Local SEO can help you get more customers. Check that your NAP is correct. Address. Your website's address and phone number. Ask satisfied customers to leave reviews and make it easier for them review your business. Without paying a fee, your chances of getting a third-party position are greater. Your website title tag should contain the keyword you want to rank. Take your time, and then search for keywords relevant to your area (e.g. "Overnight fishing Colorado"

3.2 Content Marketing: Create Thought Leadership

If you have not yet begun to create content, this should be a step in your Lead Generation Strategy. According to a survey, B2B buyers want more content from industry experts. In fact, 47% of buyers have read at least three to five pieces before engaging in sales conversations.

Garner is a pain specialist who can help with your product or services. Post blogs, news, tips and other information regularly about your industry. Visitors can also download detailed guidelines from your website. This will allow you to collect data about the people who downloaded your guides, and then enroll them in nutrition programs. They can also be engaged by sharing information about you and your products. These people could be converted into customers.

Use online marketing strategies such as SEO, Social or Email to promote your content. If people can't get it, good content doesn't matter. Organic search is the best source for quality leads, according to Farm stock. Optimize your content for search engines.

3.3 Use Off-Site SEO Techniques

An on-site strategy is only half the solution. Half of those searching online for opportunities also look on other websites. While they aren't actively searching for you online, they do spend some time browsing the web, looking at blogs and reading emails from relevant providers. 90% of online shoppers find the information that they need to make informed buying decisions. Your content is easy to find.

It can be hard to attract new visitors from other websites. It is crucial to identify your target audience, and create an online behavior profile. This profile will include what articles they read, how they use email support, what websites and groups they visit, as well as what websites they visit. You can then start reaching out to organizations that can support their mission with this information.

The community is not required that you sell anything. You are only required to offer valuable educational materials to the community. You already have many educational materials. Now you can share your materials with community managers. The manager's job is to educate and provide value for members. Now you have the same goal.

You will start to see an increase of visitors once you have enough referral assets. They will then be able get a clue about the new visitors.

3.4 Social Media is Useful

If you look at the activities on social media, it is obvious that social media isn't working. It is not the right place to publish blog articles automatically through social media. This can make it an effective tool.

Social media optimization is essential to increase traffic, engage followers, and start a conversation. It is important to ask questions, get feedback, and create creative campaigns that maximize social media sharing.

Instead of writing blog posts, start a conversation and share useful information. Engage your audience. A mini-campaign can be created that allows people download the content. Now you are sending social media access numbers to the website and inviting new users; visitors can also switch from LinkedIn to Facebook or Twitter, Instagram or Twitter to Right leads.

Social media marketing is a very profitable avenue for most businesses. Many online platforms can help you generate leads.

You can make many podcasts and play them to generate leads. These keywords will appear in Google search results if they are searched.

You can upload your product to iTunes or Sound Cloud to promote it. To increase traffic and leads, promote your products on social media or contact bloggers.

Social media is a powerful tool for digital marketing that can help increase brand visibility and awareness. As buyers search online and on social networks before buying, a strong social media presence can help build trust and loyalty. This is possible by creating business profiles on social media, personalizing them with current information about the company and then sharing it. This will make it easy for potential and existing customers to find you on their social media channels. It's as easy as that. This improves brand recognition and user experience on social media sites. Professional presence on social media can help you reach a wider audience and accomplish greater goals.

This will make it easier for loyal customers to become customers.

The increase in website traffic is another important SEO benefit from social networking marketing. You should have useful, informative and problem-solving posts on your social media accounts. Your followers will be motivated to visit your blog or site for more information or to purchase. If you share quality content via social media, you will get more traffic to your website or store. You will always have more sales opportunities if you have more people visiting the landing pages or website.

Social media can be used to generate leads. To gain leads via social networks, you must put in the effort and time to create an engaged audience. You must first decide which social media platform is right for you. Paid social ads are available on Facebook, Twitter, LinkedIn, Instagram, Pinterest and LinkedIn.

Facebook is the most used social media platform. 84% of marketers use this platform to drive traffic and create leads.

Facebook Lead Advertising is my favourite tool for Lead Generation. This format allows contacts' information to be displayed on Facebook by their contacts without leaving Facebook. Campaign strategies include "subscribe to our newsletter" or "limited time offer - 20% off your first purchase." Incentives can be offered to encourage website visitors to return to your sales funnel.

Facebook can reduce friction, lower acquisition costs, provide a better user experience and make your business more optimistic.

3.5 Optimize High Traffic Landing Page Sites

Let's now talk about leads that create leads. Leeds' primary metric is the conversion rate. It is easy to increase conversion rates and get more leads.

High-traffic landing pages are the best place to start. These pages can be optimized in a series of ways to increase or decrease their conversion rates.

Your landing page URL is the second most important element of SEO. Your URL will tell you more about the search engine page. Your URL should be consistent with the structure of your website and any other content on this page.

Your landing page title tag should always include "H1" It should describe your page and outline the proposal. You don't have to convert your keyword to this page element. Google is brilliant.

A keyword in the header without context will confuse visitors and redirect them to the search engine page. Search engines will consider a visitor clicking on your site a sign that the website has not answered their question. This qualifies your for the post.

It is important that search engine visitors can return the bounce and interest they paid for to your landing pages. If your H1 title is not the page title, it can be a great tool to drive people to your landing pages, and to increase your rank over time.

To make it easier for your visitors to understand your offers, and engage with your content, you might consider graphics, subtitles and bullet lists.

3.6 Optimize your Web Pages to Increase Conversions

Your website should be your starting point for any online lead generation efforts. It is not a good idea to get traffic from Google and social media if visitors leave your site without doing anything.

Your website should be customized to convince people to act. It is important to collect information from potential contacts, such as their name, email address, and cell phone number. This will enable you to assist them in their sales process.

How do you do it? It's possible to create a website and have it optimized immediately. There are best practices that you can use on every page of your website to increase leads.

There are many options. Lead pages allow you to create websites that are high-performing and simplify your email writing. Lead Pace lets you create and publish web pages based on a proven model for success. Lead Pace's extensive marketplace and pages templates library can help big beginners convert more leads.

3.7 Invest In New Technology and Outbound Advertising

Statistics show that inbound marketing is still more efficient than outbound. This doesn't mean that you should ignore inbound. Both of these can be combined to generate leads and increase your business.

Inbound Perspective: Personalize your emails, and get involved in online communities. Regularly address customer concerns and share informative content. This will allow you to build healthy relationships with your customers and generate more leads.

New technology is setting market trends. Smartphones are a global phenomenon. Many people access the internet and their mail via smartphones and tablets. To reach as many people as possible, your marketing efforts should focus on these devices.

To increase your chances of obtaining more leads for your business, you should be open to new technologies and channels.

Strategically use Content

Your offers can be more strategic to increase conversion rates. Different pages should be made available to different stages of the buyer's journey. All pages are necessary for understanding, thinking, and decision-making. Offers that complement these pages are also necessary.

People who contact you through the awareness page have a low conversion rate because they don't want to talk with anyone yet. If you ask them via an Awareness page, they won't respond to you asking for a demo or free trial offer. What's the reason? Demos and free trials are funnel-funnel decision making offers. It's a mistake to place them on the homepage, or any other page.

Instead, map your website so that you can determine the role of each page on the buyer's journey. Next, you can add the most relevant offers to the right pages. This will ensure you don't lose any pages during different stages of your buyer journey. If you want your visitors to have an enjoyable experience, these pages should be included.

There are many options, but not all materials are suitable for lead generation.

To generate leads for your content, you should include at most two types of content.

Traffic product content

- Lead-Generating Content

Traffic Product Content: This content will drive traffic to your website and increase your audience. Traffic is key to generating leads.

These are just a few content types you can use to generate traffic. Any of these options can be added to your content plan.

Blog Posts - These types of content are essential for any content strategy. Your blog is your hub. All content drives traffic to your blog.

Social Media Posts – These posts drive traffic back to your site.

YouTube is the second-most popular search engine for video. This is a great way to increase organic traffic to your blog over many years.

Podcasting – Encourage your guests and encourage them to share their episodes.

Infographics - To encourage social sharing, these can be added to blog posts.

Photos - It all depends upon what your business is. Your content to grow your audience will be the picture.

E-books - You can sell e-books on Amazon for free to increase your audience and drive more traffic to your website.

After you have chosen the content types you will use for traffic, you can choose your main product content.

Lead product content: Lead generation Content The content you package in Lead Magnets can be valuable and given away to anyone's address.

Lead magnets are an effective way to generate leads. It is important to give them motivation. People won't give out their email addresses to anyone.

These are the most effective content types to generate leads. This list can also be used to generate leads.

Useful Resources – These could include checklists or tools to create resource lists.

Webinars – Webinars are lead-generating leads due to their high value.

Discounts and coupons: You can provide a coupon code if you have an ecommerce business.

If you trade software, you can offer a free trial or a download.

Quiz - Your users must enter their email address to receive their quiz results.

Mini-Course : A series of emails that explain how to do something.

Free Challenge - This is a way to challenge people to overcome their obstacles and reach their goals. You can offer an open challenge for them to complete the subject in a given time. Now you have chosen the content that will be used to drive traffic and generate leads.

3.9 More compelling Bottom of the-Funnel Offers

Conversion funnels (also known as sales funnels) allow website visitors to navigate your site, ultimately leading to conversion. Your site's traffic is huge and will drop at different points. They only change a fraction of their original group. This has an impact on the size of the funnel.

Don't forget to include the seller in your offer. Get a demo, a download or a trial by contacting us. These are awesome, great, and fun. If you want to get more leads, you need to work harder.

Terrible ideas are about you. Get in touch with us to get a demo of your software and test it. Our funnel will help you reap the rewards.

You can offer value-engineering plans for the current project if you are a builder or a company in construction. This will promise to save money. Software companies need to evaluate the current process and make suggestions for improvements in embedding their software. If you are an accountant, here are six tax-saving tips that can be used to help prospects.

When it comes to people interested in learning more, is quantity more important than quality? Even if the leads are not of high quality, the goal is to fill the funnel as quickly as possible. You will need to spend more time removing non-active visitors from your website in order to increase conversion rates.

Do you have landing pages for your campaign once they have reached your page? This will allow you to control all design and copy. Your website visitor can feel invested by creating an emotional connection.

How can you do it the best?

It's not a one-size-fits all approach that will work. Customers will respond to it in a series of "quick wins".

Zappos CEO claims they have established a contact with customers from the very first phone call. This would cause Zappos to lose their understanding of the customer.

Everybody knows Zappos' legendary customer service. They put so much effort into customer satisfaction. This contact-center point is a quick victory.

Walgreens Pharmacy is another example. They listen more to their customers than they do what they want. The commute home can be time-consuming and very busy. Walgreens was the first to offer prescription pickup by drive-thru. This allowed them to streamline their sales process.

Walgreens has recently increased the shelf space for tobacco products in an effort to promote healthier lifestyles.

Walgreen printed his prescriptions in 14 languages to accommodate clients who are not English-speaking.

Walgreens issued large print editions to customers who complained about their inability read labels. He was prompt in his responses and wished for the best and most healthy eating habits. One of the most widely used exchange tracking and management systems can be optimized with paid and free (credit cards) options to suit your business's requirements. To get started, log in to your account. To open the editor, click the flag icon beside the button with the "Start/Pause experiment checkmark". This will allow to you add targets to your funnel experiment.

These plans and scenarios will make your happy. Why not share them to create sales-ready opportunities to you? Keep creating new and more creative offers until you reach your goal.

The conversion funnel is a continuous process. It is a continuous cycle, so your interactions with customers are always improving. They will not be satisfied tomorrow.

What can you do for an unforgettable experience? They exceed their expectations. They fill your conversion funnel and provide customers with a way to get to your door.

Chapter 8: Email Marketing

Easy Email Marketing Funnels

Next, set up your email marketing platform. Email marketing is an important content marketing tool that is highly effective.

It's as simple as getting peoples e-mail addresses, and then delivering the content. It's not just sales content. It also includes educational and inspirational content.

What should you do if your alarm goes off at night?

Although you might think that Instagram and Facebook are the only options, they are not used by everyone. Many people check their emails every morning as they wake up. They get messages from people they trust, and their email is more private than social media.

Let's take a look at the basics behind e-mail marketing.

The first step of the funnel is awareness. These people are people who have come to know or become aware about your work. They search Google for something, and they land at your website. Or they enter something into YouTube. They then see your video, blog article or other social media content. They are now aware of your product/service.

This is the most crucial part of the funnel. Next, we move to the next stage where less people are interested. These people spend more time looking at your content and visiting your website, which leads to a greater interest in your product. They will eventually have to make a purchase. They are making a decision about whether to purchase your product. They are hopefully being helped to make this decision and you're proving that your product can solve their problem. They then take the next step and purchase. Collaboration is essential throughout the funnel.

How does e-mail marketing help people know about you? You may have seen websites that offer "Sign Up for My Newsletter" or "Get A Free Book", or

"Subscribe to Get a Free Course, Trial or Other Benefits."

An opt-in box is where you put your email address. These opt-in forms may be used with any email marketing service that you prefer, or with other web site builders that use different plugins. WordPress is one example. If you're a web developer, you can use one of the many plugs to modify opt-in forms or create your own email opt-in boxes.

A key component of a funnel's funnel is its lead magnet. The lead magnet is something that you give in return for your email address. You could offer eBooks, discounts coupons or free trials.

It encourages people sign up to your updates and to continue coming back to your website.

After they submit their email through the opt-in form you will send them a series emails. You could send one email, but it is best to send multiple emails. Then they will get to your sales pitch. This is when they decide whether or not they want to act. This is how an email marketing channel works.

How can you get people to sign-up for your mailing list? There are two methods to get people on your mailing list.

Paid advertising and content-marketing

YouTube videos and blog posts that provide educational, interesting, and inspiring content are the basis of content marketing. Then they can go to your website and opt in.

The Next is a paid advertisement that includes Facebook ads and LinkedIn Ads. It also includes boost posts on Instagram and Facebook, where people are able to link to your page as well as access the opt in form.

Email Marketing Tools

These are our top email marketing tools. Let's start by understanding what an email marketing service actually is. You can send mass email messages to multiple people using your Yahoo or Gmail accounts. You can also send multiple emails to many people at once, ranging from hundreds to thousands.

Your account may be marked spam. You will need an actual tool to do this. These are just a few of the reasons why an email marketing tool is essential. But there are many other reasons. Automation of everything, from receiving someone's email via an opt-in webpage to automatically sending them emails. You can also segment your audience and tag them to better market to them. A lead magnet can be automatically sent to a new subscriber. This is what an email marketing services does.

The support and tools cost will also be considered. I've tried many email marketing tools and none of them are the best.

Convertkit is currently my favorite. Although there are some tools that you can use for email marketing, they are limited. They are not recommended for long-term.

MailChimp was my first choice. You can start with 2000 subscribers and 12000 electronic mails per month. It is easy to get started. It is possible to generate sales and revenue with a small list, especially if you target it with high quality.

Be a lead magnet

What are your target audiences looking for?

This is how to create a league magnet. Lead magnets are giveaways we give away to an email address. Lead magnets can be e-books from PDA Guide, an email course, series of emails, or a webinar.

It is easier to make it digital so it can be automated. It can also be downloaded online. It doesn't need any processing. To get people talking about your lead magnet, it must be of exceptional quality. I am curious about the paid content. A PDF without branding graphics is useless. It won't help anyone get any information. They won't be interested in purchasing your products or services.

Add an opt-in page to your website

You must place the Opt-In form in a way that attracts attention. The opt-in form can also be added as a popup. You can set up the popup using plugins.

To see how other people and brands present opt-in forms, you should visit websites in your niche. This will allow you to create your brand.

Segmenting and Tagging Your Audience

Before you begin building your email, it is important to segment your audience. It will be difficult to organize your email list again if you don't segment it.

Let's start by understanding why tagging is important. Tagging allows you to tag people who share similar interests, so that you can send emails to them about those topics. These emails won't get as many engagement as emails targeted at a specific group or segment of your audience.

If you have a narrow niche or only one audience, this might not work. You can tag people with different tags so that you include new visitors to your site. You might create a tag to identify customers who have purchased products from your company. This will allow you to see if they have ever spent money on your site.

You can automate the way people receive e mail sequences depending on their tag. A conversion kit allows you to create multiple sequences for people who sign up for an e-learning course. These emails will start to arrive.

Create email sequences

To allow new subscribers to get to know each other better, automated email sequences should always be sent. You can also use sequences to promote your products and services.

This is the purpose of email marketing tools. It can be done in the background, while your business is running. It doesn't matter if you send emails to specific people at specific times. You only need to choose the time and schedule the emails.

Different sequences can be created depending on your needs. Your first email could be an introduction email inviting people to visit your site. Your next email could be about new launches and your offerings. You can send the last email as a sales message, with follow-up emails.

It has been discovered that people send more emails on weekends. It could be because people have more time. Therefore, it is a good idea to test. These tools allow you to easily assess the success of your email campaigns through the click-through and open rates. This will allow you to see OK whether this email was successful.

You should verify your analytics after you have sent an email. Always test different subject lines. Choose a topic that is relevant to your product and people will be open to it.

Keep the subject brief and to-the-point, since many people access their e mails via their smartphones. The first few words are the most important.

Next, use "you". This step is crucial for any type sales copy. This is also useful for email subject lines. Emails that include the word "you" are more likely to be read. This means people are more likely open emails that contain the word "you" as their subject lines.

Next, I recommend that you use action-oriented words instead of a subject line. This will allow you to crush your competition. Write instead of Adobe After Effects tutorial on neon sign technique Adobe After Effects can be used to create your neon sign. To inspire action, use an action word in your email subject.

These people will click open emails. This theory is popular because it suggests that people fear missing out. What would you do if your favorite clothing company has a massive sale ending tonight? You will purchase the item. This is because you fear missing out.

Use all capital letters and as few exclamation points as possible. It will look spammy.

WORKSHEET: Email Marketing

What niche brands also offer Lead Magnets

What type of lead magnet would you like to create?

Which email sequences would be best for your brand?

Chapter 9: Dm Toolkits

DM Toolkits (digital market tool kits) are crucial for any online marketing strategy. These are the top tools you need to master in order to run a successful online campaign.

Google Trends and Google Keyword Planner, Ahrefs. Serpstat. SimilarWeb. Buzzsumo. Facebook Audience Insights. Facebook Ads. Google Adwords. Bing Ads. Google Analytics. Facebook Analytics for Apps. Yandex Metrica. Color Picker. Google Analytics URL.

Builder, Tag Assistant. FB Pixel Helper. Google Tag Manager. Data Scraper. Google Analytics Debugger.

These DM tools will allow you to stay on top marketing strategy.

You don't necessarily have to use all of them at once. You can choose the ones that are most effective for your campaign and then add them to your arsenal as you become more proficient with these tools.

2. technological threats

As a digital marketer, your goal should be to constantly apply new strategies and overcome technological threats to improve your marketing campaign.

You can use the DM toolkits described in the previous section, but you also have the option to use any technological devices that are available today. You are probably familiar with using computers, laptops, and other tablets to make your presence online.

9

Your phone can also be your friend. You should actually use your phone for telemarketing. You will learn all about it in the next chapter.

Online surveys are a great way to meet potential clients and to satisfy their needs. You should consider using these platforms as they are often free or very affordable.

Social media campaigns are a game changer when it comes to digital marketing. You can reach more people worldwide by using Facebook, Instagram and Twitter. You have the option to create campaigns on each platform. You can also change the settings, time and amount of funds that are allocated to a campaign at any time. You have complete control over your advertising, and can make changes at any time.

Technology threats worth keeping an eye on

1. Machine learning continues to grow

The photograph application for most phones can now detect faces and gather pictures by subject. This is an excellent case of ordinary applications that seem to be an advance in technology.

Google and other stages are being more savvy in focusing on the 'best potential client' by using machine learning. We believe this innovation will be a major breakthrough in advanced advertising. Although machine learning has been predicted by experts for a while, we expect to see it emerge in the computerized advertising world this year. Although it won't look as modern as Hollywood movies would like you to believe, it will help you achieve more by enhancing and be integrated with lots of the advanced promoting technology and usefulness that you already love. We have not seen any business move to stop referring to Artificial Intelligence as Hollywood dimension desires.

Machine learning is a powerful tool that can take some of the work out of previously work-intensive undertakings. Machine learning is a great tool for organizing and sorting out. We expect to see 10 times more machine learning being used to triage work processes and correspondences. This will allow you to think more clearly and manage some of the more complex collaborations that your office or job requires.

2. The adoption of voice search is growing.

We hope that this development in machine learning in computerized marketing tech will lead to the further development of voice inquiry, and the utilization of menial assisters by both organizations and buyers. This is especially important after devices such as Amazon Dot have been skilled for Christmas. We are also excited by the news that Apple has purchased Shazam. Apple Music will incorporate Shazam's usefulness, which we anticipate will be a rapid move to allow Shazam to benefit from Apple Music. This will not only increase its usefulness but additionally help with music suggestions based on all the information Shazam has. We expect to see an increase in voice search usage by customers. This will result in a decrease of rush hour gridlock for advertisers who have enlarging their offerings so voice look may be able to find it. This year's SEO meeting will feature interesting contextual investigations by advertisers as they investigate how to exploit voice inquiry's closest friend, 'inquiries of common English*.

3. Greater adoption of virtual reality

We also hope to see real progress in the selection and use of Virtual Reality. We anticipate this technology will be a success in the gaming industry, where it has obvious experiential benefits.

Oculus Go could be a real advantage in Virtual Reality. $199 [INR14000 approximately.] $199 [INR14000 approx.]

This is an exceptional value point considering that the simulation encounter will be completely untethered, self-working and computer generated. All augmented simulation encounters so far have been associated with expensive PC equipment. This has made it difficult to get across-the-board shopper appropriation.

This would suggest that they may have something more fundamental than a gaming stage as their primary concern in this new innovation. This is why we should question it. Drawing a 11

Correlation: It took Microsoft five years to sell 24 million units of its unique Xbox gaming platform. The record for the most gaming console units sold was held by Sony's PlayStation 2, which was released in 2000. It had an estimated 155 million units. It took Facebook eight years to reach one billion people who were allowed to access the internet. This makes it seem impossible that they could reach a similar mass of people using gaming-focused augmented simulation. This type of goal-oriented development targets would suggest a much larger use case that is more comparable to any other working framework. Perhaps not with Oculus Go, but rather with it.

Apple IOS boasts a significant portion of a half-billion clients worldwide, while Android boasts an estimated 2 billion clients. We think about whether Facebook has anything special up its sleeves beyond Oculus Go in the medium-to-long term. No matter what VR is, it will be a huge success.

This innovation will be a special gaming trick that Facebook does not want to reveal. However, we think it is worth watching as it develops and dispatches.

4. Google's display network has improved execution.

We have also been following the enthusiasm of Google for improving flag Ad understanding throughout 2017-18 as another area of progress. Google announced in June 2017 that it would include promotion blocking innovation to Google Chrome to help with weeding out poor advert encounters.

Additionally, we observed Google releasing some interesting apparatuses to inside Google look comfort in order to examine the advert experience offered by sites that highlight flag adverts. This could in general suggest that sites with poor advert experiences may experience a decrease in natural web tool execution. Although it is not certain that this will be part of Google's page ranking calculation, it would be an encouraging sign.

The Google Display Network has been experiencing serious problems for quite some time now, despite being one of the most extensive Ad arranges on Earth. Promoters have been disappointed at the large number of low-quality sites that direct into Google AdSense to make money from advertising. Control over where adverts are shown on the Google

12

The ongoing issue of Ad arrange to get indicated was a constant one. A significant buyer response has been observed with an increasing number of Ad blocking programs selections from shoppers.

According to the IAB, 26% of web clients used promotion blocking programming.

2017 saw the Coalition for Better Ads conduct research to determine which advertisement practices and organizations were most troubling individuals. It seems that Google is making an effort to improve its presentation publicizing skills. We expect that we will see an improvement in the nature of the results promoters can expect from utilizing Google Display Advertising Network. Google wants to be able to see that Advert encounter is a success.

5. Growth in Augmented Reality Apps 2019

Augmented Reality apps will see a huge increase in popularity. Apple launched an iOS toolbox to help designers assemble AR.

Applications, which will fundamentally decrease the difficulty such applications have been presenting recently. Engineers have had all winter to experiment with these devices, so we expect to see tons of AR.

Applications and amusements will soon flood into the IOS App Store and the news sections.

6. Greater use of beacon technology. It is a well-known truth that advanced deals channels are now the heart of many retail activities. Advanced properties provide a wealth of information that can be used to determine if a deal was actually out. The inquisitive truth is that people still visit physical stores. It's not easy for retailers to understand the relationship between the genuine purchasers and advanced visitors that appear to be generating the majority of the sales and income. To aid in ongoing genuine investigation, reliability plans were tied up with the mix. However, appropriation levels don't always provide enough information to fully understand the true customer connections.

13

This innovation is a great way for retailers to communicate coupons, unwaveringness and provide a wealth of information. The innovation is being explored by some advertisers to provide a continuous personalized commitment within brick and mortar stores. Beacon's innovation information could help advertisers recognize genuine Multi-channel showcasing. This is a long-held dream. The world's main area stage and the vicinity stage are managed by Unacast. They have been aggregating data from their global network of closeness sensor organisations. Their Real World Graph(tm), which includes 500 million closeness sensor organizations, is expected to be complete by 2021.

This certifiable system can confirm the area and character of clients, and it can be precise down to meters. It will undoubtedly provide a huge advantage to computerized promoting. This technology opens up a whole new world of marketing ideas that were previously only available via the internet. It pushes them into a more energizing area and sets explicit opportunities.

14

How telemarketing could be your best fit.

Telemarketing isn't a new strategy in marketing. This strategy has been around for many years. Its high efficiency is the reason it is still in use. This strategy can have a significant impact on your business. To achieve this level of success, however, you must know how to implement high-quality telemarketing campaigns..

Chapter 10: Email Marketing Reporting Metrics

The worst thing is to wait for results. Check your email provider's reports for Opens, clicks. Bounces. Unsubscribed. After you have sent an email campaign, these reports should be accessible. These reports will enable you to assess the effectiveness of your email campaigns and make adjustments for your next campaign. It's easy to create email campaigns and track the results. What does all this data mean? These are important points to keep in mind.

Your results will depend on many factors, such as how old your email list is, the time you send it, and your subject line.

The Opens

This statistic is often used to assess the effectiveness of email marketing campaigns. Open rate is the number of people who opened an email message. This is done by embedding an image into the email. A recipient opens an email asking for images.

While some email clients automatically allow images, others prompt the recipient to enable them, particularly if the sender's identity isn't known. If the recipient does not enable images, an open count cannot be calculated. Even if they have received the email, it will not be counted as open. This can be problematic at times, but the open-rate metric provides an approximate measure of a message's performance.

* Calculating an open rate: Divide the number of unique messages opened by delivered messages to calculate the open rate for an email marketing campaign. This percentage can then be used to express the number.

Calculation Method

Total number of opened emails/total sent emails

Example: 250 open/1000 send =.25 = 25

Here are some tips to help you get higher rates

Mail at least once per calendar year to keep your recipients in your thoughts.

Keep your promises and expectations high regarding content

* Use strong subject lines and preheader text to grab the attention of your recipients in an email.

* For your From label, use the company name or the person most likely to hear from you.

Clicks

The percentage of people who reply to an email message is called the click rate. This number is determined by how many people click on one message. Multiple clicks from one recipient on the same hyperlink are not considered. Click rate is not one measure. This metric depends on a variety of factors, including the nature of the calls to action, the number of links, the opt-in process, personalization, and segmentation/targeting.

Call-To-Action buttons should be included in your emails (e.g. If people see the Call-To Action buttons, they will be attracted to your emails (e.g.

There are two types click calculations.

Click rate for one link:

Calculation Method

The number of clicks on a specific link/The number of emails that were sent

Ex. Ex.

Total Links Clicked

Calculation Method

Total number clicked on each link/ Total email sent

Ex. Ex.

These are some tips for increasing clicks

* Give recipients lots of links to click
* Keep important information close to the top.
* To encourage clicks, use Call-To-Action to encourage them
* Images from the Links section
* Targeted segments within your email list will improve your chances of getting a response.

Make sure you test your email campaigns before sending them.

Social Stats

Social media is booming. This stat shows how many people have shared your email via their social media pages (e.g., Facebook or Twitter). You must include a

Social Share button to each email. You may not have access to the reports facility in all email providers.

This is done by numbers.

E.g.

Bounces

This statistic should be avoided. The bounce rate refers to the percentage of emails that are not received. A high bounce rate can lead to reputation damage and lower overall delivery rates.

There are two types of bounces: soft and harder. Soft bounces can be caused by an overly long message or when the recipient has deleted their account. Server problems can also cause soft bounces. The Internet service provider will usually try to send the message again. If they aren't resolved in a reasonable amount of time, the bounces will get more persistent. These bounces will be reclassified as hard bounces. Hard bounces can also be caused by server problems or email addresses that are not working.

Calculation Method

Total number of emails sent/Number of bounces

Ex. 100 Bounces / 1000 emails sent = 10%

These are some ways to lower your bounces

Regular mailings will help keep your list up-to-date. This will help you to stay top of mind with your recipients.

To avoid being overlooked in the event that your email address changes, make sure to include value.

* You should not sign up for more then one opt-in list.

* Members have the ability to update or unsubscribe from their preferences.

Unsubscribe

If the open rate is most viewed, the unsubscribe stat will be the least popular stat. This means that there is something wrong. This could be a sign that your content isn't relevant, that you are sending too many emails or too few, or that your list is not performing well.

Calculation Method

Total unsubscribes/Total email sent

Ex. Ex.

Tips to keep Unsubscribes Low
* Only opt-in addresses will be mailed
* Keep your mailings regular
* Let recipients know why they are getting your mails (e.g. In your email, include a note stating that the mail was sent to you because of your opt in on our website.
* Only send the requested content or promises
* Provide value

Email Marketing for LIFECYCLE
What is Lifecycle Marketing? What is Lifecycle Marketing? It is about communicating the right message to the right people at the right time. It is possible to segment customers based on their customer status, spending habits, time in your funnel, and customer status. Then, you can communicate the relevant information. You can build a deeper, more meaningful relationship by providing timely, relevant and useful information to your recipients. This will encourage signing up, purchase, subscriptions and

attendance as well as other desired actions.

You can create a Lifecycle Email Marketing Program by classifying people based on their engagement level.

1. 1.Classify your audience based on their relationship with your company.

2. 2. 2. Determine the desired goal of each recipient.

3. You can either create multiple messages or use existing messages to address each group.

Lifecycle marketing allows customers to be targeted at various stages in their relationship with your business. This allows you to make emails more efficient. You can tailor your emails to your next logical response by segmenting the audience according to their interests. Still not convinced? Let's look at how lifecycle marketing works for these three types of subscribers.

Subscriber #1: The Newbie

* Profile: This subscriber signed up for your email newsletter, and expressed interest in your company.

* Email Type: This is the email that you send to the newbie to make him feel appreciated and to encourage him to take part in the community.

* Email Goals: To encourage first purchases, to inform him about your company, promote your website, and to show him that you appreciate his support.

* Email Approach: Thank you for signing up. Give him a discount for his first order. This is a great way to inform him about all the benefits that he has to look forward to when he becomes a subscriber.

Subscriber #2: The Supporter

* Profile: This is your faithful gal who shops in your store and opens all email you send.

* Email Type: Recommend this customer to show your loyalty and provide the VIP treatment. Make him feel appreciated and he will be more inclined to recommend you.

* Email Goals: Encourage higher buying, exceptional customer service, and loyalty

* Email Approach: Offer sneak peeks of future sales, discounts to valued

customers and target email creation based on viewing history. Send abandoned cart reminders, provide customer support, and respond immediately when needed.

Subscriber #3: The Bystander

* Profile: This is an older member of your email list, but they haven't made any recent purchases. They might also not be able to open or click on any of your emails.

* Email Type: Regain subscriber loyalty with special offers, and "we missed" messages

* Email Goals: Help him understand and start reengagement.

* Email Approach: Contact us to ask for feedback via social media, surveys or other means. Make the person feel valued by offering incentives for site visits and purchases.

Segmenting your customers based on customer behavior is the basis of lifecycle marketing. You can then create targeted emails to encourage participation.

Chapter 11: Top Digital Marketing Tips to Grow Your Business

Digital marketing is a vast field. Over the years, digital light terminology has expanded to include email marketing, social media marketing, and content marketing.

Each month, over 300,000.00 people search for the keyword "digital market". This is a huge search volume, if you ask me.

Either you are a new owner of a business or a digital marketer who has the savvy to increase sales through digital marketing.

This scenario is possible. Imagine you are the owner of a small brick and mortar clothing shop. Television, radio and newspaper advertising can help grow your business. It is possible. But not in the same way as the iMac. Advertising costs can be prohibitive and you may not know if your message has reached the right people.

Digital marketing is an excellent way to reach people outside your immediate area. You can control how your online marketing campaigns are run with a data-driven platform. This platform allows you to gather information about potential customers, and use it to your advantage.

I'm sorry if you are just starting an online marketing campaign but feel stuck. Most likely, you don't have all the digital marketing tools that your business needs to grow.

4.1 Mobile Friendly Experience For Users

Did you know that more than half of all website traffic comes from mobile searches? Customers can check reviews, compare prices, and make online purchases using mobile devices. Jacksonville SEO is an essential component of digital marketing strategies. Mobile optimization is becoming more important. It is a smart idea to make your website mobile-friendly. This might be something you'd also like:

On a mobile version of your website, text should only appear once

- Make sure the button to call-to-action is clearly visible

- The buttons must be large enough for clickability and interactivity.

Devices popping up on mobile devices are very disturbing. They must be reduced.

Site should load quickly. Consider integrating Accelerated Mobile Pages technology (AMP). AMP websites load in 0.5 seconds on Google. It's incredible!

Visitors will enjoy a better user experience with compress files.

Mobile-friendly Testing Tools — Regularly test your website with mobile-friendly testing tools

After you have created your mobile marketing strategy, it is crucial to monitor your mobile metrics. Your mobile policy updates must support your decisions, just like any marketing decision. It is crucial to analyze your mobile analytics when developing and maintaining your mobile strategy. Google Analytics can provide marketers with all the information they need to delight customers.

Engagement metrics are an excellent place to start when looking at mobile matrices. Mobile users are more prevalent than desktop users. Even if your mobile traffic is the highest, we can still verify the success of your mobile strategy.

- Bounce Rate (and Adjusted Boncing Rate)
- Pages per session
- Soft and hard exchange

Mobile site speed

Page path

The Opening Page

High-Performance ecommerce products

Now you can compare mobile metrics with desktop metrics to see the differences. The expanded data from Google Analytics can be used to notify marketers of any changes that may require content types such as mobile site/app design, usability and usability.

However, this doesn't mean that an image will look better on a desktop computer. Original equipment can make mobile rendering easier. Mobile-friendly websites are not always the best. Make sure you check your mobile pages. Although the page is considered poor on mobile devices, it still looks great on all devices.

It is crucial to verify how close buttons and links are to each other. Because of my large hands, it is hard for me to click the right link when I am focused. It would be great if your mobile app/website didn't have any functions. By making it as easy as possible for users to do what they want, users will be able make the most of their experience. Include A//B testing to get the most information possible about your website/app. Google offers great tips on designing a mobile website.

Mobile is essential. Mobile strategy and analytics are crucial to providing a better customer experience. Mobile marketing is a must for marketers. Mobile technology is always changing, so marketers must keep up to date with the latest information in order reach their target audience. If the market offers the best mobile experience then I don't need a computer on my desktop.

4.2 Increase Social Media Presence

Social media should be used to promote your business and increase your reach. Studies show that businesses should be tweeting at least 15 times per week. If you are a business owner, it is likely that you don't have time to log in to all your social media accounts. It is therefore important to choose the right tool.

You can save time by scheduling posts and remain active on social media. Buffer lets you manage all of your social media accounts in one place. You can schedule posts in advance, pick a time when they are most popular, then analyze their performance. Tools can be used to improve your social media presence.

Customer support is possible through social media. Customers are now using social media to solve problems. Customers no longer have to wait for companies to respond to their emails or call them. They can now wait up to several days. Customers prefer social messaging channels to email or phone customer service.

Instead of focusing solely on selling, try to help people. You can use your social media platform as a customer support platform. This will allow you to reach more people and solve problems. You can create a Facebook chatbot that answers your questions even if you're not there. If customers feel that they can solve their problems quickly, they will purchase from you.

Social media marketing is a great opportunity for your business. Social media marketing is not about creating a Twitter, Instagram or Facebook account. Social media is crucial to boosting your marketing efforts. It might be possible.

- Awareness raising

Marketing your brand

Visibility online: Increased visibility

Engage your audience

Attract potential customers

Are you still talking to people who don't reply to your messages? They may be right. Users won't interact with you on social networks if they don't get something in return. It is essential to engage with your followers on social media.

If you want to increase your social media presence, your social media accounts should be made a social network. Any comments left on your posts must be responded to. Posts can answer questions. Customers and followers can be thanked for sharing user-generated content. Connecting with your customers and building real relationships will increase your social media presence.

Email Marketing: 4.3

Have you ever opened a marketing email without being able to identify the company? It doesn't contain a sales pitch or story and might not be compatible with their website. Sometimes it is not their fault. They check their email on a computer but forget that their email is mobile. It's not displayed correctly. This tool opens most emails. Many companies don't realize the benefits of email marketing and are unaware of them.

Two main principles underpin digital strategy and email marketing: a personal website and great, mobile-friendly emails. Email marketing is the most effective way to market digitally and offers the highest ROI. You can also access a constant stream of content to keep in touch with customers. 94% of people use emails. It's easy to use, fast and personal. Customers can have the best selection and most personalized options. They also have the ability to track their performance.

Brand strategy: Awareness, Communication, and Conversion. The goal of top brand marketing is to increase awareness. The perception of customers and their knowledge can be affected by email frequency, distribution, content and knowledge. Engaging customers with your mission, brand message, or brand goals will increase brand appreciation and loyalty.

Email on Acid states email is still a key tool for business communication. It is crucial to establish relationships with customers. Send a welcome email and personalize your content. Re-engage customers by telling stories. Engage customers and keep them engaged throughout the journey. This goes beyond marketing. Consumers want to feel connected to a trusted brand that is respected and has a large audience.

Your emails are the ultimate goal of the CTA.

What type of email should you send?

Your emails represent your brand's personality. It is crucial to choose the best email marketing type for your company in order not to damage your brand. Hub Spot's 2016 survey found that 78% unsubscribe to promotional emails. This is due to the fact that brands send too many emails. It is important to know what your potential customers and customers want from your emails. Email marketing goes beyond selling. Email marketing strategies must include a balance between transaction, communication and trigger emails.

Brands trust the rule of "70/20/10" for acid emails. 70% of emails contain tips, advice, and educational presentations. 20% should "focus exclusively on thought-leaders' content, and your list should give them the impression that you offer exclusive access to their ideas," while 10% should focus on the product. This rule states that customers must feel valued and have meaningful relationships.

Email marketing, if done correctly, can be one of digital marketing's most powerful elements. Check your email records to see the number of opened cold emails. It's not hard to see why. Headlines aren't interesting, boring, and clickable. Email marketing should get customers to click on your emails. No matter how valuable your content is, if it fails to click, it will be tossed into the trash and left to rot. Your readers will be drawn to your pain points. This will help you increase click-through rates tremendously.

Influencer Marketing

Influencer marketing can be described as selling hot cakes online. Marketing is a complex process that digital marketers need to influence. It is important to choose an influencer who has a strong social media presence. ADVOCACY is the key to marketing success.

Influencers can easily get their products or services by just paying for them. It is important to be honest and authentic in your marketing. Make sure that influencers align with your goals and beliefs when choosing them. If they aren't, you don't have the right to make your product/service famous.

It is crucial that you set goals and establish key performance indicators (KPIs) before you start your search for influencers who will sponsor your brand. These metrics will allow you to decide the best marketing strategy for your company and how to optimize it.

It's a great way for you to reach your audience and introduce your brand. You can increase customer engagement by selecting the platform that is most popular in your target market.

If you create campaigns on the wrong platform, you will waste time and money. Research is essential before making any decision. By mapping out all details, you can avoid any errors and get positive results.

You can find out the most active areas of your audience and where they are most likely. This topic is important because it will draw their attention to your content.

If you don't know your target audience, it is difficult to endorse products that appeal. Reach out to gaming influencers and ask them to endorse beauty products. They won't be interested in the proposals of any other person in their network, regardless of how large or small.

These people are also called your buyer persona. They can provide the best information and help you understand your ideal customer's needs, problems, and preferences. They will help you reach your goals faster so you can get results quickly.

Influencer marketing is a growing trend that gives businesses more followers, revenue and engagement. This is a great way to get your audience to notice your business and encourage growth. To ensure that you can use this method to grow the business, it is crucial to do your research in advance.

4.5 Video Marketing

Video is the easiest media format to digest. Are you noticing video posts the most prominently on your Facebook feed?

Video marketing isn't a new trend. People prefer to watch videos than read product information. Customers watch four times more videos than they read about products.

Videos can be a great way for users to stay on your site longer. This can be a positive influence on search engine rankings (residence time ranking factor).

Your website can be enhanced by a well-made video. It allows visitors to navigate their products and services.

Digital marketing agencies face the greatest challenge of all: creating a strong pipeline that is filled with quality leads.

Find out what your chances are of getting emails from sales reps. This is a great way to build a relationship with sales reps and stand out from the rest.

Send a video explaining how you are improving the sales process of agencies selling to local businesses.

Video testimonials can be a powerful CRO tool in an agency environment.

After you've researched the agencies, take a look at their website. He or she will be able give their opinion during the recorded video testimonials. Instantly you will feel more confident, and credible.

Clients face many logistical challenges when recording these videos, downloading video recording software, and then recording the video before downloading a file.

It is unlikely that customers will be able perform a task efficiently, especially if they don't have the right tech skills.

Video is a powerful tool for capturing the SOPs digital marketing agencies use to manage their businesses. Our agency is not an exception.

Sometimes we record videos as well as tasks in Google Docs. This is done to supplement written instructions. This especially important when you are performing complex multi-step tasks such as installing Google Tag Manager onto customer sites.

Sometimes it is the best way of teaching is to show how to do it in a video.

Engaging social video content can be created by digital marketing agencies to maintain their presence on social media. These videos won't use stock images, but other videos that relate to the products.

These are some video marketing tips that will help you tell the story of your business more effectively.

Focus on simple messages that are easy-to-understand when you call for action.

You can add a character to your story by talking directly to the viewer about the script.

Highlight Your Script With Startup: The Setup; the Middle - Where you introduce a problem; the Conclusion – Here's how to fix the problem (alongside a solution for your business).

Make the viewer feel called to action.

Data Analytics The Focus

Competitivity is only possible if digital marketers are data-driven. Google Analytics is well-known. However, there are many other online tools like Mix Pal or

Heap Analytics that can help you understand your historical data and explain its workings to maximize your ROI on your marketing campaigns.

Instapage and similar tools include temporal attention and heatmaps to help you gain a better understanding of your visitors in order to generate more leads.

This is convenient and useful when you consider the fact that 58% of the Aberdeen reports will include the best-in-class analytics tool for marketers. This is not the time to shoot arrows at the board in the hope they stick, regardless of the method you use.

Setting milestones for Your Business without the right information is guesswork. You should not let your business goals change over time. Analytics can be a great tool to help you.

Analytics allows you to collect data about past trends and activities. Once you have a clear idea of your goals you can begin to make them. This will enable you to take advantage of all opportunities that could help your business grow. This is especially important if you have specific goals. Data analysis can help you identify your strengths and weaknesses. This can be very useful in helping you grow your company.

Analytics can help you divide your audience into various groups. This will allow you to avoid unnecessary content and increase your business' value.

This will enable you to make better products and personalize your communications. Google Analytics can be used to help you understand your audience. It is a tool that can be used for analysing search queries that lead to your website. This allows you to understand what your customers want. If you know what your audience wants, you will be able satisfy their needs.

Analysing tools provide more detail about what people think of your brand. Social media allows you to track brand mentions and hashtags. Social media platforms offer analytics that can help you track the reach and effectiveness of your advertising campaigns. This provides data about your audience's interests, and their origins. These platforms give you demographic information as well as tell you which tools are being used by your audience. These data can be used to improve your website and manage content.

To help you in the future, you can analyse and gather information about online trends to aid your planning. Analytics is a great way to reach millions of people via social media. This will enable you to convert more customers and increase traffic as your business grows.

There are obvious benefits to compiling data within your business. Analytics tools can be added to your website to provide functional insight. Track different activities to generate actionable data.

It's becoming harder to believe that "we can't measure them". Analytics is what will make you feel lost. Analytics and data are key to understanding your company's strengths and limitations.

Analytics should be an integral part of your company's success at every stage. You can achieve this by investing in the best equipment and appointing qualified staff. Encourage all employees in your company to use data to make informed decisions. Analytics can be applied to all levels of your business, which will result in increased revenue and profitability.

4.7 Use landing pages to keep up-to-date with the most recent marketing techniques

A visitor clicking on your ad can make or break your campaign. A landing page is often the first impression prospects get of your company. Optimize your landing page's message, call-to-action, and other elements to maximize your advertising ROI.

The customized search ad's message match and fixed features create a unique ad experience that users will love.

Message matching refers to the process of comparing the content of an advertisement with that on a landing page so that the message is reinforced in future minds and remains relevant.

One notable tip for digital marketing is to stay up-to-date on the latest trends in your industry. Facebook recently launched new creative ads that are engaging and dynamic. What's the latest addition to Amazon advertising?

Hacking is a rising trend. You don't need to know everything in order to make a deal with customers or business partners.

Marketing is not difficult. There are many resources that can help. These seven blogs are related to growth and you can share valuable information on a regular basis to get started.

Marketing - The Land of Marketing

- Kiss metrics

Content Marketing Institute

Search Engine Land

Digital Marketer

- Social Media Examiner

- Moz

4.8 High Quality Content

With the popularity of social media platforms to reach potential customers, quality content is more important than ever. High-quality content encourages people to share positive reviews about products and services. Quality content for a long time has been praised as the best way to promote someone's products or services in 2020.

Digital marketing is built on high quality content. Creativity and productivity are the keys to creating high-quality, original content. Digital marketing is about creating valuable and relevant content that can be linked to on merit.

If you are able to create timeless, high-quality content that is easily shared across all channels, it will be possible. Many brands have a solid content strategy. They also keep it updated. Most of their social media posts are based upon content that they created for their website.

Because it can generate links on merit, high quality is a powerful digital marketing tool. These are backlinks. If your content is high-quality and timely, backlinks are not difficult to earn. These links are essential for spreading your work and attracting readers. This will eventually lead you to conversion and traffic.

Although it may seem like a long-term strategy, this is actually a shorter-term strategy that takes less time. Websites with quality content will have a better reputation and rank higher on search engines. This gives you security, and peace of mind. Natural links are reliable, long-lasting, and reliable.

4.9 Voice Search Optimization

Given the popularity of smart devices such as Alexa and Google Home Business, they need to optimize their content to include voice searches. Searches can be based on the language spoken or typed by people. Text-based search engine optimization is what you call search engine optimization. This includes voice.

Voice search is the future for online marketing. Voice search is the future for online marketing. It's not possible to reach your target audience and achieve your growth goals without optimizing your voice search marketing.

Digital marketing is always evolving, and positive trends are emerging. Voice search is one of the most popular trends. It's easy to see why voice search is so popular.

Voice search should be used by every business to improve their visibility. Voice search is an innovative way to put SEO to work.

Voice questions are more conversational than text queries. Voice questions are much more conversational than text because the user is talking to search engines rather than typing text.

Voice queries tend to be local content. It is more common for users to search "near me", on their mobile phones, than other people. This is also a common way they search by speaking. Native SEO is important in optimizing for viewing.

Consumers expect instant gratification. Voice search is a way to get instant gratification. They can use voice search to check the business listings instead of visiting the websites.

Conversational queries are crucial when optimizing voice search results. Customers prefer to ask Google directly for answers to their questions. Your content should allow users to ask questions directly. It can be difficult for your content to reach a targeted audience if you don't answer users' questions.

If you want to create answer-focused content, it is important that you include the right keywords in your content. You must consider the intent of your users. You can do this by walking in the shoes of your users. They will find it easier to identify keywords they most likely search for. This will allow you to generate keywords quicker and more accurately.

Keywords are searched by buyers simply by typing text. They avoid long-tail keywords. Keywords that are easily used in voice searches can be a great way of finding keywords. Your content should contain many keywords. Include keywords in your content.

A query can be used to ask voice searchers for information about products or services. Google might be asked by the customer to tell them "Hey Google! This is the best restaurant I've ever eaten at." Prioritize the "who", "what", and "why" aspects of your product when deciding your focus keywords.

If you want voice search to be more efficient, it's smart to include a FAQ page. It is simple. You can have both a question answer and a query-word. This content will enhance your user experience and improve your SEO ranking. This strategy should be part your voice optimization strategy.

Another tip is to only use natural language when improving your online presence. It's the language that people use every day. It allows the voice to sound natural regardless of whether the material is blog content, website content, or social media posts. You would be more useful if you spoke directly with your audience member.

Optimizing for voice is best. Prioritize relevance over all other strategies when optimizing. Relevance is critical when a customer searches your business. Search engines ensure that customers get the most relevant results. This is crucial for their success.

While it can seem time-consuming, good optimization will deliver tangible results over the long-term for your company. This trend will only continue to grow. Companies that fail to innovate their SEO strategies risk losing all their organic traffic.

4.10 Additional Chatbots

Artificial intelligence is a key area. Chatbots are used on websites. This technology represents a major advancement in artificial intelligence technology. Chatbots are able to help with issues such as Cortana. They can also be used in instant messaging conversations like Facebook Messenger. Chatbots are able to quickly respond to potential customers, without waiting for an answer.

Chatbots for service, also known by brand chatbots are a great way to improve customer services and increase your business's performance. These chatbots are able to improve customer service, optimize marketing strategies and gather feedback from customers. They can also be used for increasing customer satisfaction.

Marketing is all about customer satisfaction. Customer satisfaction is essential. Customers need you to be available 24 hours a day to answer their queries. Chatbots make it possible, even though it may seem impossible from a human standpoint. This will let your customers know that you are always available and ready to help them.

Marketers need to remember that customers are more comfortable using messaging to communicate with them than they are reading for hours. Chatbots allow businesses to easily integrate communication strategies into their marketing plans. Chatbots are able to help businesses save money while making it easily accessible to customers 24 hours per day.

Chatbots are getting more sophisticated and can offer valuable information about customers. This information includes customer buying habits, interactions with brands and engagement with your website. This data is useful to companies because it can be used for personalizing future marketing campaigns. These data can be used to solve customer problems and personalize shopping experiences.

Chatbots can also create customized ads. Chatbots can learn more about customers and collect basic information when they interact with them. These data can be used to create customized ads. This clever ad seeks assistance. This ad seems to indicate that the customer is getting more support than sales.

Chatbots can be created to gather insights from customers. SurveyBot allows you to send surveys once a task is completed. This includes registrations, downloads, purchases, and many other tasks. Your Messenger bot can receive a study bot-generated link at any time. You can use the chatbot's data to create a customized message that guides customers and helps in increasing conversion rates.

Chapter 12: Pay per Click

PPC (pay per click) is an internet marketing model where publicists promote their products and services on the publisher's website. Publicists are paid when a client clicks on the promotion. This is an example internet marketing, which involves buying visits from clients to a website.

Pay-per-click usually associates with the first-level webindices, such as Google Ads and Bing Ads. Sponsors often offer catchphrase phrases that relate to their target market for web crawlers. Instead of using an offering framework, content destinations are charged a fixed price per view. PPC "show" ads, also known as standard promotions, appear on sites that contain related substances. These ads are not paid-per click publicizing. To the promotion models for interpersonal organizations such as Facebook and Twitter, pay-per-click was added.

Websites may also be able to offer PPC ads. Websites that use PPC ads will show a commercial when a watchword query coordinates with a publicist's catchphrase list. These notices are also called supported connections or supported ads. They appear in the web crawler results pages, or wherever a web developer decides to display them on a substance website.

Although the PPC publicizing model can be used to mistreat click-misrepresentation, Google and other companies have implemented mechanized frameworks that prepare for clicks from degenerate web developers or contenders.

Principal Purpose

Pay-per-click (or expense per impression) is combined with pay-per-click to evaluate internet marketing's viability and effectiveness. Pay-per-click, which is cheaper than expense per impression and provides information about how effective publicizing was, is better. To gauge interest and consider clicks. Pay-per-click is the preferred measure if the promotion's primary purpose is to get people to click on a link or direct them towards a goal. After a certain amount of impressions, click-through rates will drop and pay-per-click will increase.

8.1- PPC TERMINOLOGY

Below is a list of common terms that are used in PPC advertising. A brief description follows.

Ad group

A whole collection of keywords can be found under one name. Maximum 20,000 keywords can be found under the same name.

Ad Network

An Ad Network is an online company which coordinates sponsors for websites that promote products. Promotion systems are dealers for both the suppliers (locales with substance that can promote, such as tutorialspoint.com), and the buyers (the publicists). Websites can use advertising systems to avoid having to set up promotion servers and follow programming.

Ad Position

The ad position is the order in which advertisements are displayed on a website.

Ad Rank

It is used for measuring the Ad Proposition.

Call-To-Action (CTA)

This marketing term refers to the action that a visitor desires on a website.

Campaign

It could be described as a collection relevant advertising groups.

Click-Through Rate

It is the number of times that a visitor clicks on an ad from a user after viewing it. It can also be used to indicate the number of clicks per 1000 impressions. CTR contributes to Ad Rank.

Conversion

Conversion is the action the user takes after clicking on an ad. Conversion is when a visitor does a certain action.

Conversion Rate

It's the measure of the success of a paid crusade. It is calculated based on how many guests perform the ideal activity (e.g. filling a structure, purchasing an item).

Cost per Action

It is the cost you pay per lead, sign-up, or purchase. Also known as cost per acquisition

Cost per click

This means you will pay a fixed amount per click on the ads.

Cost Per Mille (CPM)

It is the price paid for every thousand views of the PPC ad.

URL Destination

It is the address you wish the user to land upon clicking the ad.

Geo-targeting

Geo-targeting allows ads to be delivered to specific geographic areas. Publicists have the option to choose which areas they wish to place their ads.

Impression

Internet publicizing refers to the percentage of advertisements that are seen and not clicked on. Each promotion it displays is only one impression.

Catchphrase

It is asked by a client to follow him. It's a combination of words or words that a client enters into the search box. The internet searcher coordinates your watchwords and returns significant results on Search Engine Results Page (SERP).

Point of arrival

It is any website that is different from the main website where the guest is located. Negative Keywords are keywords you do not want your promotion to appear on.

PPC Bid

This is the maximum amount a promoter will spend on a click.

Prospect

Prospect is a potential client who can purchase an item/administration that has been publicly advertised.

Qualitative Score

It is a powerful measure that you can use for determining the nature of your promotions and watchwords. It is used to determine the nature of your advertisement and watchword. A high score indicates strong support for promotion rank.

Internet searcher result page. (SERP).

This page displays all results that an internet searcher returned in response to a client's query.

Split Testing

This is a great way to test an advertisement to see if it can be used in a PPC promotion.

8.2 - HISTOLOGY

Only a few sites claim to be the first online PPC model. In the late 1990s, many others were created. Planet Oasis was the first and most well-known PPC variant. It was launched in 1996. Ark Interface II was a Packard Bell NEC Computers division that created this work area application. It connected to educational as well as business websites. The "pay-per-visit" Ark Interface II model was met with skepticism by business organizations. The agreement included 400 brands paying $0.05 to $0.25 per click plus a fee for position.

Jeffrey Brewer, a 25-representative representative business representative, presented Goto.com to the TED gathering in February 1998. (later Overture, now part Yahoo!), presented a pay per click web index verification of idea at the TED gathering in California. This introduction, and subsequent events, created the PPC publicizing framework. The creation of the PPC model is often credited to Bill Gross, the author of Idealab and Goto.com.

Google started web index promotion in December 1999. Only October 2000 saw the introduction of AdWords, which allows promoters create content ads to be placed on Google's search engine. PPC was introduced in 2002. Promotions were charged at cost per 1,000 impressions (CPM), until then. Google may have filed a patent encroachment suit claiming that the adversary search administration exceeded its limits using its advertisement placement apparatuses.

Yahoo! PPC was first introduced by GoTo.com in 1998. Yahoo! Yahoo! [14] Before this point, Yahoo's primary source for SERPs promotion was the logical IAB publicizing Unit (mostly 468x60 show ads). Yahoo! Yahoo! Yahoo! Yahoo! Yahoo! announced that it will acquire Overture for

$1.63 billion. ValueClick and adMarketplace offer PPC administrations, in addition to AdWords and AdCenter.

Google Ads (in the past Google AdWords), Microsoft adCenter and Yahoo! PPC suppliers are the most prominent. Search Marketing was the largest operator of PPC systems, with all three operating on an offer-based basis. In 2014, PPC (Adwords), also known as internet publicizing, was responsible to around USD 45 Billion of the total USD 66 Billion Google's annual revenue. In 2010, Yahoo and Microsoft combined their efforts against Google, and Microsoft's Bing was used by Yahoo to list its items. After they merged, their PPC stage was renamed AdCenter. BingAds, their system of outsider sites that allows AdCenter promotions for content or pennant advertisements to populate their site's page with.

8.3- Search Engine Advertising

Search Engine Advertising (SEA), one of the most well-known types of PPC marketing, is a popular option. Publicists may offer promotions to clients by supporting them to connect to an internet searcher. Clients scan for watchwords that relate to an item or administration. After a client clicks on an advertisement, the connection takes the client to the item's website. Google requires that the item or specialist pay a fee. Appealing promotions are key to attracting clients to your PPC battle. Sponsors should be aware of the following tips when creating an online advertisement:

* Look for catchphrases that are compatible with an administration or item.

* Selecting the most relevant keywords

* Combining keywords relevant

* Web indexes pay less per click for ads that are important and useful by arranging keywords. Publicists get more business in return for their efforts. Google AdWords, for example, is a popular promoting platform. It allows companies to place ads on Google's search engine.

PPC Advertising

These entities are involved in PPC Advertising

* Product or service seller

* PPC Advertiser

* Provider of landing pages

* Landing Page

8.4 How a PPC Ad is Worked Out

Here is the process for creating a PPC ad

1. Advertisers create an account online, load it with money (e.g. Rs 15000), Many companies have a PPC budget that can range from hundreds to thousands of rupees per month to millions.

2. 2. 2. The advertiser creates an ad with a brief text. PPC ads may include images in some cases.

3. 3. The advertiser will provide a list of keywords associated with the ad.

4. Advertisers decide how much they will pay per click on an advertisement.

5. 5.

6. 6.

7. Clicking on an advertisement will take you to the advertiser's website. Clicks must be paid by the advertiser.

General Formula to Calculate PPC

To calculate PPC, use the following formula:

Pay per click ($) = Advertising cost ($) / Ad clicks

PPC Advantages

PPC is a great tool for branding and lead generation.

Rapid action

PPC is a great way to get huge traffic and fast results. PPC also allows for faster branding and more buzz. PPC results are much quicker than SEO results, which can take several months or even years to fully materialize.

An initial investment is very small.

For creating an account or inserting a PPC ad, search engines don't charge fees. The user is only charged if someone clicks on their ad.

Instant Results

When quality ads are posted, PPC ads can provide faster responses than SEO methods.

8.5- Flat Rate PCP

Flat-Rate PPC is an agreement between the advertiser and publisher on a fixed amount to be paid per click. Publishers set a rate which determines the cost per Click or CPC depending on the difficulty of the term. This means that clicks will be paid for by other people.

The cost of terms like "Austin TX PPC", and "PPC Austin TX", will depend on the number of websites that use these keyphrases to direct their visitors to their locations. Another assurance is the cost of website content. It will cost more per click-through if you have higher quality visitors. Publishers can be negotiated lower rates, especially if they have a long-term contract with high-esteem.

This rate structure is especially common on value-search websites like PriceGrabber or eBay, which often offer rates for specific watchwords and expressions.

These are not the best areas to advertise. Advertisers will spend more to place their location at the top of the page. These locations are broken down into administration and item classes. These areas give you a greater chance of finding a buyer from them. Buyers who are further along in the buying process will have a better understanding of what they require.

8.6- Bid-based PPC

Bid-based PPC lets advertisers compete with other advertisers in a network like Google AdWords or Microsoft AdCenter. Advertisers decide the maximum amount they are willing to pay for promotion spots. It all depends on the catchphrase. The promotion is clicked by a guest.

All bids that contain the watchword, which focuses on the geo-area where the searcher is located, as well as the date and time of each hunt are evaluated and determined to be the winner. Advertisements may appear in multiple spots, which is quite normal. There may be several spots for advertisements. In these cases, the total bids determine the position of the champs. While the most prominent advertisement is the one with the highest bid, quality factors like promotion quality can also be important.

These real publicizing networks go beyond promotion spots on SERPs. These networks also have connections to outsider destinations, which allow for logical advertisements to be placed in a similar way as on web journals. These destinations are not web crawlers, but outsiders. Web journals, for example, can sign up to receive advertising in the promotion network. These websites are sometimes referred to as substance network. These advertisements are logic ads because the catchphrases used relate to the page's setting.

Google Display Network promotions generally have a lower click-through rate (CTR) and lower conversion ratio (CR), than regular internet searcher ads. These can still be a great source of optional payment for publishers and a cheap way to publicize.

You have two options: either you can hire someone to manage your PPC battles, or you can automate it using a bid administration framework. This will improve achievement and scale. This is a great way for these frameworks to be made more well-known.

8.7 Innovative Methods to Increase Pay Per Click Campaigns

This industry is always changing, so make sure you do your research.

Be sure to choose the right keywords

PPC ads allow you to bid on keywords that match your advertisement. Your bid's viability depends on many factors, including how much you spend. It is therefore important that you only bid on the correct keywords.

The Keyword Planner is a powerful tool that helps you find the most relevant keywords for Google AdWords. Although this is a great place to start, it's important that you remember that other people may be able get similar keywords from Google.

It is possible that you are falling for a keyword that your competitors aren't bidding on.

Lead with value first to prevent plagiarism

This strategy works in all marketing areas and is also very effective for PPC.

Keywords should be focused on details and representations of the product.

However, the actual promotion copy should adopt a value-based strategy.

Do not create duplicates that portray your administrations to be a "web-based marketing organisation", but instead highlight the strengths and benefits of you administrations such as "increase traffic," "develop conversions," "improve impressions."

Both Newcomers and Old-Hands are equally important

You're familiar with the concept and operation of the marketing channel.

PPC campaigns are focused on building intrigue and mindfulness. By using keywords, they target people who don't know about your business.

The final stages of the marketing pipeline are those who know what companies like yours offer, and they have a goal to purchase. Keywords are a good option for individuals in the responsibility phase (e.g. "contract online life supervisory group")

The closer you are to your goal, the more likely your promotion watcher is to reach it.

Concentrate your Ad Groups

Some will argue that it is wrong to bid on keywords with red dots. This is a smart decision. This is a smart move.

Anybody who recognizes your image can visit your website legally. To get there, they don't have to spend money on promotion. If you have items that are not in competition with other brands you should bid on those keywords.

Do not bid if you are a Peugeot vehicle dealer. Bid on "Peugeot vehicles available for sale." This allows you to meet people looking for certain items, but also gives you the opportunity to make connections with them.

Don't cut clicks that don't convert.

Your PPC advertisement may be seen by many people even though they might not be the client you are trying to market to.

Let's go back to the vehicle seller model. Your ads should not be visible to anyone searching for Mazda car sellers if you only sell Peugeot cars. Negative keyword modifiers can be used to ensure that your advertisement isn't visible in immaterial searches. You might assign "Mazda", one of your negative keywords, to this position.

It is also important to forbid specific keywords. You should not offer "free" negative keywords, except if you are providing a preliminary. People may look for organizations similar to yours in order to find work. Negative keywords like "business", work, enlisting and "profession" are good options if you don't want to procure.

You should keep structuring your negative keywords list for a while. This will help you avoid spending money on clicks that don't convert.

#7 - Choose Who Sees Your Ads

Remember that not everyone will click on your advertisement and use your service.

Click extortion refers to clicking on PPC ads by rivals in order make a profit but not receiving anything.

This could lead to an increase in the cost of your PPC campaigns. IP Exclusion is a way to find IPs that click on your promotions but do not change. This will ensure that your promotion is not visible to them in the future.

It is essential to test different entry points. It is important to place your CTA in the right spot, use the right image, and write the right heading. These factors can make a big difference in the conversion rate of a greeting page.

#8 - Create different ad groups for mobile

As you create responsive content, responsive PPC ads should be created for mobile clients. You can also include photos and recordings if you use internet-based PPC.

These media ads don't necessarily bring down businesses, so clients who have flexibility won't click them. You can compare portable promotion bids to work area ads. You can make ads less likely to show on mobile, or even completely prevent them from showing up. Mobile promotions can also be made.

It's time to get it right

Time is as important as the location. It is easy to see that online business clients can work at different times and days of the week.

They won't be able to change their mind if they don't want to see your website Monday morning. They might be more willing to spend money Saturday night and put in more effort.

You can choose the day and time that your advertisement will appear from many PPC stages. They can run for up to three weeks. After you have achieved the highest traffic and conversions then reduce your timeframe.

This helps to avoid wasteful bidding and ensures that people only click when they have the chance and desire to become customers.

Ads are not as important as landing pages.

Advertisements for explicit items or administrations should not be ignored. They will lead you to your landing page.

It is important to make it easy for potential clients to convert from looking at your advertisement to becoming customers.

To promote your promotional bouquets, you can use individual greeting pages.

These pages should be filled with substance and encourage the client to act. You might have one page for Mitsubishi cars and one for Peugeot cars if you are selling vehicles. Each company should have its own advertising gathering. Your potential clients could give up if you put obstacles in their path.

It is crucial to test different points of entry in order to make sure they are as effective as possible. It is important to choose the right location for your CTA and use the correct photo.

Conclusion

We hope that you found useful information to help improve your online business and personal brand. We tried to provide every strategy and tool that you could need to make your digital business a cash-making machine.

Now, it's up to you to put into practice the lessons you have learned. Remember that understanding a concept is not the same as making it work for yourself. As an entrepreneur, influencer or entrepreneur, you must always be open to trying new strategies.

If you are serious about your digital marketing strategy, we are certain that you will be ahead of the competition. It is no secret that many businesses are sloppy when it comes to digital marketing. You will be miles ahead of your competitors and have a greater chance of gaining an advantage over them in the long-term.

We encourage you to share the valuable information you have found in this book with others who might be interested in digital advertising. Never forget to share is caring.